BIRDER'S
LIFE LIST & DIARY

BIRDER'S
LIFE LIST & DIARY

edited by STEVEN C. SIBLEY

revisions by RICHARD E. BONNEY, JR.,
and DANIEL OTIS

 CORNELL LABORATORY OF ORNITHOLOGY
SAPSUCKER WOODS, ITHACA, NY

PREFACE

When Frank Chapman initiated the first Christmas Bird Count in 1900 and suggested that people observe birds with binoculars rather than shotguns, few would have imagined the popularity that bird watching would come to hold in North America. By the 1950s excellent field guides to North American birds had become widely available, along with high-quality binoculars that most people could afford.

In 1959, Roy and Betty Dietert published an innovative book designed to help the growing ranks of American birders keep track of the birds they had seen. Called the *Birder's Life List and Diary*, it was the first such book ever published. The Dieterts continued to publish it for 26 years, making constant revisions to reflect changes in the names and distributions of birds that visit North America.

In 1985 Roy and Betty decided they could publish their book no longer. They offered the Cornell Laboratory of Ornithology the opportunity to continue their labor of love, and with pride we accepted the challenge, revising their latest edition to make it more accurate and versatile than ever.

We and the Dieterts wish you fine birding and hope this book will come to hold many happy memories.

ACKNOWLEDGMENTS

Many people helped to make this project possible. I thank Roy and Betty Dietert, who provided the rights to their book as well as their time and encouragement during the revision. Roger Tory Peterson generously granted permission for his Yellow-bellied Sapsucker to grace the cover.

I also thank several staffers at the Cornell Laboratory of Ornithology, particularly Charles R. Smith, Jill Crane, and Richard E. Bonney, Jr., who provided helpful comments and suggestions. And I owe special thanks to Maureene Stangle for word processing the entire contents of this book.

Most of all, I am indebted to Rosalie Borzik, who handled every aspect of production, from design and layout to printing.

S.C.S.

PREFACE TO THE SECOND EDITION

Between the time the first edition of this book was printed in 1986 and the time it sold out in 1990, the Committee on Classification and Nomenclature of the American Ornithologists' Union had changed the names of certain bird species, recognized some new species, and documented still others as new but regular visitors to North America. The second edition has been revised to reflect these changes. Special thanks to Kevin McGowan, curator of the Cornell University bird collection, for his technical assistance, and to Kirstie Forbes-Robertson, manager of the Crow's Nest Birding Shop at the Lab of Ornithology, for coordinating production.

R.B. and D.O.

THE CORNELL LABORATORY OF ORNITHOLOGY

Birds are the business of the Cornell Lab of Ornithology, an international center for the study, appreciation, and conservation of birds. Our mission: to develop, apply, and share the tools for understanding and protecting birds. To do this we monitor bird populations, collect and analyze bird sounds, and publish research results. We also link bird watchers to professional ornithologists by encouraging birders to participate in our research programs. The Laboratory was founded in 1917 and is a nonprofit unit of Cornell University, primarily supported by memberships and grants.

Our **Bird Population Studies** program enlists a huge network of volunteer observers to monitor North American bird populations. Information obtained by this program benefits researchers, conservation organizations, wildlife management agencies, and ultimately the birds themselves. One of our best-known efforts is Project FeederWatch, a continentwide survey of birds at backyard feeders performed by thousands of kitchen-window volunteers.

Our **Library of Natural Sounds** contains the world's largest collection of bird songs, over 60,000 recordings that represent more than half the world's species. Sounds archived in the library are used for research and to produce top-quality records, tapes, and CDs, such as the *Peterson Field Guide to Bird Songs*.

The **Bioacoustics Research Program** is the investigative arm of the Library of Natural Sounds. Using advanced computer systems, bioacoustics staffers analyze sounds to understand how and why animals communicate.

Our **Education and Information Services** provide instructive publications, programs, and activities. These include *Living Bird* magazine; summer field courses; color slides and slide sets; a home study course in bird biology; *BirdWatch*, a nationally syndicated radio program; and tours to birding hot spots around the world.

Our **Sanctuary and Observatory** are located in the 200-acre Sapsucker Woods wildlife sanctuary on the outskirts of Ithaca, New York. Four miles of trails wind through woodlands and swamps filled with nesting and migrating birds. Headquarters is the Lyman K. Stuart Observatory, where picture windows overlook a specially designed bird-feeding garden and a 10-acre pond. On permanent exhibit is an extensive collection of original paintings by the renowned bird artist, Louis Agassiz Fuertes.

Our **Crow's Nest Birding Shop,** through its retail store and mail-order catalog, offers the finest in birding books, gear and gifts—everything you need to enjoy birds and bird watching. Each item in the shop is carefully selected in consultation with our professional ornithologists.

The Cornell Lab of Ornithology is a membership organization. All members receive our quarterly magazine, *Living Bird,* along with discounts on items purchased from our birding shop and invitations to participate in our courses and tours. To join, fill out the membership form in the back of this book, or write or call: CLO, Membership Department, 159 Sapsucker Woods Road, Ithaca, New York 14850. (607) 254-2425.

For a free copy of the Crow's Nest Birding Shop catalog, please write or call: Crow's Nest, CLO, 159 Sapsucker Woods Road, Ithaca, New York 14850. (607) 254-2400.

TABLE OF CONTENTS

iv   Preface/Acknowledgments

vi   The Cornell Laboratory of Ornithology

vii   Table of Contents

1   Introduction

3   Quick-Search Guide

5   Species Listing

163   Appendix A—Hawaiian Species

178   Appendix B—Accidental Species

182   Appendix C—Life List

191   Index

INTRODUCTION

A life list is a compilation of all the bird species you have seen during your lifetime and the date and location where you first saw them. Such a list provides an excellent way of retaining memories of birding adventures. It can also help you learn more about birds—by looking for new species, you will quickly learn what time of year various birds are present in your area, and in what habitats and geographic locations they are usually found.

This book includes 934 bird species, all those known to occur in North America north of Mexico as well as species that regularly appear in Hawaii. Because some birders keep track of all the distinct plumages of birds they have seen, we have even listed 27 birds that were formerly considered distinct species but are now classed as subspecies, color forms, or color morphs of other species.

Our list was compiled from the 6th edition of the American Ornithologists' Union *Check-List of North American Birds* (1983) and subsequent supplements (1985, 1987, and 1989). As a result, some of the species' names included here will not match those used in field guides published prior to 1989.

Now for an explanation of the parts of this book.

QUICK-SEARCH GUIDE

This feature will help you find the pages on which a particular group of birds is listed. Simply locate the group (for example, bluebirds) within the black bars on the Quick-Search Guide, then turn to the pages on which the black edging lines up with that bar.

SPECIES LISTING

This section, the majority of the book, contains a listing of the 697 bird species found regularly in North America north of Mexico. The 27 birds that were formerly considered distinct species are also included; their names are printed within quotation marks.

All species are listed in taxonomic order, the same order used in most field guides. If you have trouble locating a species, check the Index or use the Quick-Search Guide on page 3.

Within the listing, space is provided for entering the date and location of your first sighting of each species. You might also consider recording the habitat in which the bird was seen, notes on the bird's behavior, or anything else you'll want to remember.

Space for recording accidental species—those that do not occur regularly in North America—is provided at the end of most bird groups.

HAWAIIAN SPECIES (Appendix A)

This appendix lists the 74 species that are seen regularly in the Hawaiian Islands but have never been recorded in North America north of Mexico. These species are listed taxonomically and are included in the Index but not in the Quick-Search Guide.

ACCIDENTAL SPECIES (Appendix B)

Listed here are 163 species that appear very rarely in North America but whose occurrence has been officially accepted by the Committee on Classification and Nomenclature of the American Ornithologists' Union. Several columns are provided for checking off any of these species that you see and for listing the page numbers on which you have recorded information about the sightings.

LIFE LIST (Appendix C)

Many folks who keep a life list enjoy remembering which species was seen first, which was number 100, and so on. Appendix C is a convenient format for recording your list in the order in which the birds were seen.

INDEX

This section is an alphabetical index of all the birds listed in the book, including the 27 subspecies that were formerly considered full species. We have provided 12 columns adjacent to each name; these are designed for keeping year, state, yard, or other lists. Please note: all hyphenated names, such as Screech-Owl and Wood-Peewee, are considered one word. Therefore, Screech-Owl and Wood-Pewee are listed alphabetically under "S" and "W" rather than Owl or Pewee.

Gaviiformes	Loons
Podicipediformes	Grebes
Procellariiformes	Albatross, Shearwaters, Storm-Petrels
Pelecaniformes	Boobies, Pelicans, Cormorants
Ciconiiformes	Bitterns, Herons, Egrets, Ibises
Phoenicopteriformes	Flamingo
Anseriformes	Swans, Geese, Ducks
Falconiformes	Vultures, Osprey, Kites, Hawks, Falcons
Galliformes	Pheasant, Grouse, Turkey, Quail
Gruiformes	Rails, Coots, Limpkin, Cranes
Charadriiformes	Shorebirds
	Jaegers, Skuas, Gulls, Terns, Skimmer,
	Alcids
Columbiformes	Pigeons, Doves
Psittaciformes	Parrots
Cuculiformes	Cuckoos, Roadrunner, Anis
Strigiformes	Owls
Caprimulgiformes	Nighthawks, Goatsuckers
Apodiformes	Swifts, Hummingbirds
Trogoniformes	Trogon
Coraciiformes	Kingfishers
Piciformes	Woodpeckers
Passeriformes	Flycatchers, Larks, Swallows
	Jays, Crows, Chickadees, Titmice, Nuthatches, Creeper
	Wrens, Kinglets, Gnatcatchers
	Bluebirds, Thrushes, Mockingbird, Thrashers
	Pipits, Waxwings, Shrikes, Starling
	Vireos, Warblers
	Tanagers, Cardinals, Grosbeaks, Buntings
	Towhees, Sparrows, Longspurs
	Blackbirds, Orioles
	Finches, Crossbills, Weaver Finches

RED-THROATED LOON

Gavia stellata

DATE

LOCATION

REMARKS

ARCTIC LOON

Gavia arctica

DATE

LOCATION

REMARKS

PACIFIC LOON

Gavia pacifica

DATE

LOCATION

REMARKS

COMMON LOON

Gavia immer

DATE

LOCATION

REMARKS

YELLOW-BILLED LOON

Gavia adamsii

DATE

LOCATION

REMARKS

PODICIPEDIFORMES

GREBES

	DATE	
LEAST GREBE	LOCATION	
Tachybaptus	REMARKS	
dominicus		

	DATE	
PIED-BILLED	LOCATION	
GREBE		
	REMARKS	
Podilymbus podiceps		

	DATE	
HORNED GREBE	LOCATION	
Podiceps auritus	REMARKS	

	DATE	
RED-NECKED	LOCATION	
GREBE		
	REMARKS	
Podiceps grisegena		

	DATE	
EARED GREBE	LOCATION	
Podiceps nigricollis	REMARKS	

7

WESTERN GREBE *Aechmophorus occidentalis*	DATE
	LOCATION
	REMARKS

CLARK'S GREBE *Aechmophorus clarkii*	DATE
	LOCATION
	REMARKS

	DATE
	LOCATION
	REMARKS

	DATE
	LOCATION
	REMARKS

	DATE
	LOCATION
	REMARKS

8

PROCELLARIIFORMES

ALBATROSS, FULMAR, PETRELS, SHEARWATER

BLACK-FOOTED ALBATROSS *Diomedea nigripes*	DATE
	LOCATION
	REMARKS

NORTHERN FULMAR *Fulmarus glacialis*	DATE
	LOCATION
	REMARKS

BLACK-CAPPED PETREL *Pterodroma hasitata*	DATE
	LOCATION
	REMARKS

MOTTLED PETREL *Pterodroma inexpectata*	DATE
	LOCATION
	REMARKS

CORY'S SHEARWATER *Calonectris diomedea*	DATE
	LOCATION
	REMARKS

9

SHEARWATERS

**PINK-FOOTED
SHEARWATER**

Puffinus creatopus

DATE	
LOCATION	
REMARKS	

**FLESH-FOOTED
SHEARWATER**

Puffinus carneipes

DATE	
LOCATION	
REMARKS	

**GREATER
SHEARWATER**

Puffinus gravis

DATE	
LOCATION	
REMARKS	

**BULLER'S
SHEARWATER**

Puffinus bulleri

DATE	
LOCATION	
REMARKS	

**SOOTY
SHEARWATER**

Puffinus griseus

DATE	
LOCATION	
REMARKS	

SHEARWATERS, STORM-PETREL

SHORT-TAILED SHEARWATER	DATE
	LOCATION
	REMARKS
Puffinus tenuirostris	

MANX SHEARWATER	DATE
	LOCATION
	REMARKS
Puffinus puffinus	

BLACK-VENTED SHEARWATER	DATE
	LOCATION
	REMARKS
Puffinus opisthomelas	

AUDUBON'S SHEARWATER	DATE
	LOCATION
	REMARKS
Puffinus lherminieri	

WILSON'S STORM-PETREL	DATE
	LOCATION
	REMARKS
Oceanites oceanicus	

FORK-TAILED STORM-PETREL *Oceanodroma furcata*	DATE
	LOCATION
	REMARKS

LEACH'S STORM-PETREL *Oceanodroma leucorhoa*	DATE
	LOCATION
	REMARKS

ASHY STORM-PETREL *Oceanodroma homochroa*	DATE
	LOCATION
	REMARKS

BLACK STORM-PETREL *Oceanodroma melania*	DATE
	LOCATION
	REMARKS

LEAST STORM-PETREL *Oceanodroma microsoma*	DATE
	LOCATION
	REMARKS

PELECANIFORMES

TROPICBIRDS, BOOBIES

| WHITE-TAILED TROPICBIRD

Phaethon lepturus	DATE
	LOCATION
	REMARKS

| RED-BILLED TROPICBIRD

Phaethon aethereus	DATE
	LOCATION
	REMARKS

| MASKED BOOBY

Sula dactylatra	DATE
	LOCATION
	REMARKS

| BLUE-FOOTED BOOBY

Sula nebouxii	DATE
	LOCATION
	REMARKS

| BROWN BOOBY

Sula leucogaster	DATE
	LOCATION
	REMARKS

NORTHERN GANNET *Morus bassanus*	DATE
	LOCATION
	REMARKS

AMERICAN WHITE PELICAN *Pelecanus erythrorhynchos*	DATE
	LOCATION
	REMARKS

BROWN PELICAN *Pelecanus occidentalis*	DATE
	LOCATION
	REMARKS

GREAT CORMORANT *Phalacrocorax carbo*	DATE
	LOCATION
	REMARKS

DOUBLE-CRESTED CORMORANT *Phalacrocorax auritus*	DATE
	LOCATION
	REMARKS

14

CORMORANTS, ANHINGA

OLIVACEOUS CORMORANT Phalacrocorax olivaceous	DATE
	LOCATION
	REMARKS

BRANDT'S CORMORANT Phalacrocorax penicillatus	DATE
	LOCATION
	REMARKS

PELAGIC CORMORANT Phalacrocorax pelagicus	DATE
	LOCATION
	REMARKS

RED-FACED CORMORANT Phalacrocorax urile	DATE
	LOCATION
	REMARKS

ANHINGA Anhinga anhinga	DATE
	LOCATION
	REMARKS

MAGNIFICENT FRIGATEBIRD *Fregata magnificens*	DATE
	LOCATION
	REMARKS

	DATE
	LOCATION
	REMARKS

	DATE
	LOCATION
	REMARKS

	DATE
	LOCATION
	REMARKS

	DATE
	LOCATION
	REMARKS

CICONIIFORMES

BITTERNS, HERONS, EGRET

AMERICAN BITTERN *Botaurus lentiginosus*	DATE
	LOCATION
	REMARKS

LEAST BITTERN *Ixobrychus exilis*	DATE
	LOCATION
	REMARKS

GREAT BLUE HERON *Ardea herodias*	DATE
	LOCATION
	REMARKS

"GREAT WHITE" HERON *(subspecies of Great Blue Heron)*	DATE
	LOCATION
	REMARKS

GREAT EGRET *Casmerodius albus*	DATE
	LOCATION
	REMARKS

SNOWY EGRET	DATE
Egretta thula	LOCATION
	REMARKS

LITTLE BLUE HERON	DATE
Egretta caerulea	LOCATION
	REMARKS

TRICOLORED HERON	DATE
Egretta tricolor	LOCATION
	REMARKS

REDDISH EGRET	DATE
Egretta rufescens	LOCATION
	REMARKS

CATTLE EGRET	DATE
Bubulcus ibis	LOCATION
	REMARKS

HERONS, IBISES

GREEN-BACKED HERON *Butorides striatus*	DATE
	LOCATION
	REMARKS

BLACK-CROWNED NIGHT-HERON *Nycticorax nycticorax*	DATE
	LOCATION
	REMARKS

YELLOW-CROWNED NIGHT-HERON *Nyctanassa violacea*	DATE
	LOCATION
	REMARKS

WHITE IBIS *Eudocimus albus*	DATE
	LOCATION
	REMARKS

GLOSSY IBIS *Plegadis falcinellus*	DATE
	LOCATION
	REMARKS

IBIS, SPOONBILL, STORK, FLAMINGO

WHITE-FACED IBIS *Plegadis chihi*	DATE
	LOCATION
	REMARKS

ROSEATE SPOONBILL *Ajaia ajaja*	DATE
	LOCATION
	REMARKS

WOOD STORK *Mycteria americana*	DATE
	LOCATION
	REMARKS

GREATER FLAMINGO *Phoenicopterus ruber*	DATE
	LOCATION
	REMARKS

	DATE
	LOCATION
	REMARKS

ANSERIFORMES

WHISTLING-DUCKS, SWANS

FULVOUS WHISTLING-DUCK *Dendrocygna bicolor*	DATE
	LOCATION
	REMARKS

BLACK-BELLIED WHISTLING-DUCK *Dendrocygna autumnalis*	DATE
	LOCATION
	REMARKS

TUNDRA SWAN *Cygnus columbianus*	DATE
	LOCATION
	REMARKS

TRUMPETER SWAN *Cygnus buccinator*	DATE
	LOCATION
	REMARKS

MUTE SWAN *Cygnus olor*	DATE
	LOCATION
	REMARKS

GREATER WHITE-FRONTED GOOSE *Anser albifrons*	DATE	
	LOCATION	
	REMARKS	

SNOW GOOSE *Chen caerulescens*	DATE	
	LOCATION	
	REMARKS	

"BLUE" GOOSE *(color morph of Snow Goose)*	DATE	
	LOCATION	
	REMARKS	

ROSS' GOOSE *Chen rossii*	DATE	
	LOCATION	
	REMARKS	

EMPEROR GOOSE *Chen canagica*	DATE	
	LOCATION	
	REMARKS	

GEESE

BRANT *Branta bernicla*	DATE
	LOCATION
	REMARKS

"BLACK" BRANT *(subspecies of Brant)*	DATE
	LOCATION
	REMARKS

CANADA GOOSE *Branta canadensis*	DATE
	LOCATION
	REMARKS

	DATE
	LOCATION
	REMARKS

	DATE
	LOCATION
	REMARKS

WOOD DUCK *Aix sponsa*	DATE
	LOCATION
	REMARKS

GREEN-WINGED TEAL *Anas crecca*	DATE
	LOCATION
	REMARKS

"COMMON" TEAL *(subspecies of Green-winged Teal)*	DATE
	LOCATION
	REMARKS

AMERICAN BLACK DUCK *Anas rubripes*	DATE
	LOCATION
	REMARKS

MOTTLED DUCK *Anas fulvigula*	DATE
	LOCATION
	REMARKS

DABBLING DUCKS

MALLARD
Anas platyrhynchos

DATE	
LOCATION	
REMARKS	

"MEXICAN" DUCK
(subspecies of Mallard)

DATE	
LOCATION	
REMARKS	

NORTHERN PINTAIL
Anas acuta

DATE	
LOCATION	
REMARKS	

BLUE-WINGED TEAL
Anas discors

DATE	
LOCATION	
REMARKS	

CINNAMON TEAL
Anas cyanoptera

DATE	
LOCATION	
REMARKS	

NORTHERN SHOVELER

Anas clypeata

DATE	
LOCATION	
REMARKS	

GADWALL

Anas strepera

DATE	
LOCATION	
REMARKS	

EURASIAN WIGEON

Anas penelope

DATE	
LOCATION	
REMARKS	

AMERICAN WIGEON

Anas americana

DATE	
LOCATION	
REMARKS	

DATE	
LOCATION	
REMARKS	

DIVING DUCKS

CANVASBACK *Aythya valisineria*	DATE
	LOCATION
	REMARKS

REDHEAD *Aythya americana*	DATE
	LOCATION
	REMARKS

RING-NECKED DUCK *Aythya collaris*	DATE
	LOCATION
	REMARKS

TUFTED DUCK *Aythya fuligula*	DATE
	LOCATION
	REMARKS

GREATER SCAUP *Aythya marila*	DATE
	LOCATION
	REMARKS

LESSER SCAUP *Aythya affinis*	DATE
	LOCATION
	REMARKS

COMMON EIDER *Somateria mollissima*	DATE
	LOCATION
	REMARKS

KING EIDER *Somateria spectabilis*	DATE
	LOCATION
	REMARKS

SPECTACLED EIDER *Somateria fischeri*	DATE
	LOCATION
	REMARKS

STELLER'S EIDER *Polysticta stelleri*	DATE
	LOCATION
	REMARKS

SEA DUCKS

HARLEQUIN DUCK *Histrionicus histrionicus*	DATE	
	LOCATION	
	REMARKS	

OLDSQUAW *Clangula hyemalis*	DATE	
	LOCATION	
	REMARKS	

BLACK SCOTER *Melanitta nigra*	DATE	
	LOCATION	
	REMARKS	

SURF SCOTER *Melanitta perspicillata*	DATE	
	LOCATION	
	REMARKS	

WHITE-WINGED SCOTER *Melanitta fusca*	DATE	
	LOCATION	
	REMARKS	

29

COMMON GOLDENEYE

Bucephala clangula

DATE
LOCATION
REMARKS

BARROW'S GOLDENEYE

Bucephala islandica

DATE
LOCATION
REMARKS

BUFFLEHEAD

Bucephala albeola

DATE
LOCATION
REMARKS

SMEW

Mergellus albellus

DATE
LOCATION
REMARKS

HOODED MERGANSER

Lophodytes cucullatus

DATE
LOCATION
REMARKS

MERGANSERS, STIFF-TAILED DUCKS

COMMON MERGANSER

Mergus merganser

DATE

LOCATION

REMARKS

RED-BREASTED MERGANSER

Mergus serrator

DATE

LOCATION

REMARKS

RUDDY DUCK

Oxyura jamaicensis

DATE

LOCATION

REMARKS

MASKED DUCK

Oxyura dominica

DATE

LOCATION

REMARKS

DATE

LOCATION

REMARKS

VULTURES, OSPREY, KITE

BLACK VULTURE *Coragyps atratus*	DATE	
	LOCATION	
	REMARKS	

TURKEY VULTURE *Cathartes aura*	DATE	
	LOCATION	
	REMARKS	

CALIFORNIA CONDOR *Gymnogyps californianus*	DATE	
	LOCATION	
	REMARKS	

OSPREY *Pandion haliaetus*	DATE	
	LOCATION	
	REMARKS	

HOOK-BILLED KITE *Chondrohierax uncinatus*	DATE	
	LOCATION	
	REMARKS	

KITES, EAGLE

AMERICAN SWALLOW-TAILED KITE *Elanoides forficatus*	DATE
	LOCATION
	REMARKS

BLACK-SHOULDERED KITE *Elanus caeruleus*	DATE
	LOCATION
	REMARKS

SNAIL KITE *Rostrhamus sociabilis*	DATE
	LOCATION
	REMARKS

MISSISSIPPI KITE *Ictinia mississippiensis*	DATE
	LOCATION
	REMARKS

BALD EAGLE *Haliaeetus leucocephalus*	DATE
	LOCATION
	REMARKS

NORTHERN HARRIER

Circus cyaneus

DATE	
LOCATION	
REMARKS	

SHARP-SHINNED HAWK

Accipiter striatus

DATE	
LOCATION	
REMARKS	

COOPER'S HAWK

Accipiter cooperii

DATE	
LOCATION	
REMARKS	

NORTHERN GOSHAWK

Accipiter gentilis

DATE	
LOCATION	
REMARKS	

DATE	
LOCATION	
REMARKS	

34

BUTEOS

COMMON BLACK-HAWK *Buteogallus anthracinus*	DATE ___ LOCATION ___ REMARKS ___

HARRIS' HAWK *Parabuteo unicinctus*	DATE ___ LOCATION ___ REMARKS ___

GRAY HAWK *Buteo nitidus*	DATE ___ LOCATION ___ REMARKS ___

RED-SHOULDERED HAWK *Buteo lineatus*	DATE ___ LOCATION ___ REMARKS ___

BROAD-WINGED HAWK *Buteo platypterus*	DATE ___ LOCATION ___ REMARKS ___

SHORT-TAILED HAWK
Buteo brachyurus

DATE	
LOCATION	
REMARKS	

SWAINSON'S HAWK
Buteo swainsoni

DATE	
LOCATION	
REMARKS	

WHITE-TAILED HAWK
Buteo albicaudatus

DATE	
LOCATION	
REMARKS	

ZONE-TAILED HAWK
Buteo albonotatus

DATE	
LOCATION	
REMARKS	

RED-TAILED HAWK
Buteo jamaicensis

DATE	
LOCATION	
REMARKS	

BUTEOS, EAGLE

"HARLAN'S" HAWK (color form of Red-tailed Hawk)	DATE
	LOCATION
	REMARKS

FERRUGINOUS HAWK Buteo regalis	DATE
	LOCATION
	REMARKS

ROUGH-LEGGED HAWK Buteo lagopus	DATE
	LOCATION
	REMARKS

GOLDEN EAGLE Aquila chrysaetos	DATE
	LOCATION
	REMARKS

	DATE
	LOCATION
	REMARKS

CRESTED CARACARA *Polyborus plancus*	DATE
	LOCATION
	REMARKS

AMERICAN KESTREL *Falco sparverius*	DATE
	LOCATION
	REMARKS

MERLIN *Falco columbarius*	DATE
	LOCATION
	REMARKS

APLOMADO FALCON *Falco femoralis*	DATE
	LOCATION
	REMARKS

PEREGRINE FALCON *Falco peregrinus*	DATE
	LOCATION
	REMARKS

FALCONS

GYRFALCON *Falco rusticolus*	DATE
	LOCATION
	REMARKS

PRAIRIE FALCON *Falco mexicanus*	DATE
	LOCATION
	REMARKS

	DATE
	LOCATION
	REMARKS

	DATE
	LOCATION
	REMARKS

	DATE
	LOCATION
	REMARKS

PLAIN CHACHALACA *Ortalis vetula*	DATE
	LOCATION
	REMARKS

GRAY PARTRIDGE *Perdix perdix*	DATE
	LOCATION
	REMARKS

BLACK FRANCOLIN *Francolinus francolinus*	DATE
	LOCATION
	REMARKS

CHUKAR *Alectoris chukar*	DATE
	LOCATION
	REMARKS

RING-NECKED PHEASANT *Phasianus colchicus*	DATE
	LOCATION
	REMARKS

GROUSE, PTARMIGANS

	DATE	
SPRUCE GROUSE	LOCATION	
Dendragapus canadensis	REMARKS	

	DATE	
BLUE GROUSE	LOCATION	
Dendragapus obscurus	REMARKS	

	DATE	
WILLOW PTARMIGAN	LOCATION	
Lagopus lagopus	REMARKS	

	DATE	
ROCK PTARMIGAN	LOCATION	
Lagopus mutus	REMARKS	

	DATE	
WHITE-TAILED PTARMIGAN	LOCATION	
Lagopus leucurus	REMARKS	

RUFFED GROUSE *Bonasa umbellus*	DATE
	LOCATION
	REMARKS

SAGE GROUSE *Centrocercus urophasianus*	DATE
	LOCATION
	REMARKS

GREATER PRAIRIE-CHICKEN *Tympanuchus cupido*	DATE
	LOCATION
	REMARKS

LESSER PRAIRIE-CHICKEN *Tympanuchus pallidicinctus*	DATE
	LOCATION
	REMARKS

SHARP-TAILED GROUSE *Tympanuchus phasianellus*	DATE
	LOCATION
	REMARKS

42

TURKEY, QUAIL

WILD TURKEY *Meleagris gallopavo*	DATE	
	LOCATION	
	REMARKS	

MONTEZUMA QUAIL *Cyrtonyx montezumae*	DATE	
	LOCATION	
	REMARKS	

NORTHERN BOBWHITE *Colinus virginianus*	DATE	
	LOCATION	
	REMARKS	

SCALED QUAIL *Callipepla squamata*	DATE	
	LOCATION	
	REMARKS	

GAMBEL'S QUAIL *Callipepla gambelii*	DATE	
	LOCATION	
	REMARKS	

CALIFORNIA QUAIL

Callipepla californica

DATE

LOCATION

REMARKS

MOUNTAIN QUAIL

Oreortyx pictus

DATE

LOCATION

REMARKS

DATE

LOCATION

REMARKS

DATE

LOCATION

REMARKS

DATE

LOCATION

REMARKS

GRUIFORMES

RAILS

YELLOW RAIL *Coturnicops noveboracensis*	DATE
	LOCATION
	REMARKS

BLACK RAIL *Laterallus jamaicensis*	DATE
	LOCATION
	REMARKS

CLAPPER RAIL *Rallus longirostris*	DATE
	LOCATION
	REMARKS

KING RAIL *Rallus elegans*	DATE
	LOCATION
	REMARKS

VIRGINIA RAIL *Rallus limicola*	DATE
	LOCATION
	REMARKS

SORA *Porzana carolina*	DATE
	LOCATION
	REMARKS

PURPLE GALLINULE *Porphyrula martinica*	DATE
	LOCATION
	REMARKS

COMMON MOORHEN *Gallinula chloropus*	DATE
	LOCATION
	REMARKS

AMERICAN COOT *Fulica americana*	DATE
	LOCATION
	REMARKS

CARIBBEAN COOT *Fulica caribaea*	DATE
	LOCATION
	REMARKS

LIMPKIN, CRANES

LIMPKIN *Aramus guarauna*	DATE
	LOCATION
	REMARKS

SANDHILL CRANE *Grus canadensis*	DATE
	LOCATION
	REMARKS

WHOOPING CRANE *Grus americana*	DATE
	LOCATION
	REMARKS

	DATE
	LOCATION
	REMARKS

	DATE
	LOCATION
	REMARKS

BLACK-BELLIED PLOVER	DATE	
Pluvialis squatarola	LOCATION	
	REMARKS	

LESSER GOLDEN-PLOVER	DATE	
Pluvialis dominica	LOCATION	
	REMARKS	

SNOWY PLOVER	DATE	
Charadrius alexandrinus	LOCATION	
	REMARKS	

WILSON'S PLOVER	DATE	
Charadrius wilsonia	LOCATION	
	REMARKS	

SEMIPALMATED PLOVER	DATE	
Charadrius semipalmatus	LOCATION	
	REMARKS	

48

PLOVERS, OYSTERCATCHERS

PIPING PLOVER

Charadrius melodus

DATE	
LOCATION	
REMARKS	

KILLDEER

Charadrius vociferus

DATE	
LOCATION	
REMARKS	

MOUNTAIN PLOVER

Charadrius montanus

DATE	
LOCATION	
REMARKS	

AMERICAN OYSTERCATCHER

Haematopus palliatus

DATE	
LOCATION	
REMARKS	

BLACK OYSTERCATCHER

Haematopus bachmani

DATE	
LOCATION	
REMARKS	

BLACK-NECKED STILT *Himantopus mexicanus*	DATE
	LOCATION
	REMARKS

AMERICAN AVOCET *Recurvirostra americana*	DATE
	LOCATION
	REMARKS

GREATER YELLOWLEGS *Tringa melanoleuca*	DATE
	LOCATION
	REMARKS

LESSER YELLOWLEGS *Tringa flavipes*	DATE
	LOCATION
	REMARKS

SOLITARY SANDPIPER *Tringa solitaria*	DATE
	LOCATION
	REMARKS

WILLET, TATTLER, SANDPIPERS, CURLEW

| WILLET

*Catoptrophorus
semipalmatus*	DATE
	LOCATION
	REMARKS

| WANDERING
TATTLER

Heteroscelus incanus	DATE
	LOCATION
	REMARKS

| SPOTTED
SANDPIPER

Actitis macularia	DATE
	LOCATION
	REMARKS

| UPLAND
SANDPIPER

*Bartramia
longicauda*	DATE
	LOCATION
	REMARKS

| ESKIMO
CURLEW

Numenius borealis	DATE
	LOCATION
	REMARKS

WHIMBREL

Numenius phaeopus

DATE	
LOCATION	
REMARKS	

BRISTLE-THIGHED CURLEW

Numenius tahitiensis

DATE	
LOCATION	
REMARKS	

LONG-BILLED CURLEW

Numenius americanus

DATE	
LOCATION	
REMARKS	

BLACK-TAILED GODWIT

Limosa limosa

DATE	
LOCATION	
REMARKS	

HUDSONIAN GODWIT

Limosa haemastica

DATE	
LOCATION	
REMARKS	

GODWITS, TURNSTONES, SURFBIRD

BAR-TAILED GODWIT

Limosa lapponica

DATE	
LOCATION	
REMARKS	

MARBLED GODWIT

Limosa fedoa

DATE	
LOCATION	
REMARKS	

RUDDY TURNSTONE

Arenaria interpres

DATE	
LOCATION	
REMARKS	

BLACK TURNSTONE

Arenaria melanocephala

DATE	
LOCATION	
REMARKS	

SURFBIRD

Aphriza virgata

DATE	
LOCATION	
REMARKS	

RED KNOT *Calidris canutus*	DATE
	LOCATION
	REMARKS

SANDERLING *Calidris alba*	DATE
	LOCATION
	REMARKS

SEMIPALMATED SANDPIPER *Calidris pusilla*	DATE
	LOCATION
	REMARKS

WESTERN SANDPIPER *Calidris mauri*	DATE
	LOCATION
	REMARKS

RUFOUS-NECKED STINT *Calidris ruficollis*	DATE
	LOCATION
	REMARKS

SANDPIPERS

LEAST SANDPIPER *Calidris minutilla*	DATE
	LOCATION
	REMARKS

WHITE-RUMPED SANDPIPER *Calidris fuscicollis*	DATE
	LOCATION
	REMARKS

BAIRD'S SANDPIPER *Calidris bairdii*	DATE
	LOCATION
	REMARKS

PECTORAL SANDPIPER *Calidris melanotos*	DATE
	LOCATION
	REMARKS

SHARP-TAILED SANDPIPER *Calidris acuminata*	DATE
	LOCATION
	REMARKS

PURPLE SANDPIPER

Calidris maritima

DATE	
LOCATION	
REMARKS	

ROCK SANDPIPER

Calidris ptilocnemis

DATE	
LOCATION	
REMARKS	

DUNLIN

Calidris alpina

DATE	
LOCATION	
REMARKS	

CURLEW SANDPIPER

Calidris ferruginea

DATE	
LOCATION	
REMARKS	

STILT SANDPIPER

Calidris himantopus

DATE	
LOCATION	
REMARKS	

SANDPIPERS, DOWITCHERS, SNIPE

BUFF-BREASTED SANDPIPER *Tryngites subruficollis*	DATE
	LOCATION
	REMARKS

RUFF *Philomachus pugnax*	DATE
	LOCATION
	REMARKS

SHORT-BILLED DOWITCHER *Limnodromus griseus*	DATE
	LOCATION
	REMARKS

LONG-BILLED DOWITCHER *Limnodromus scolopaceus*	DATE
	LOCATION
	REMARKS

COMMON SNIPE *Gallinago gallinago*	DATE
	LOCATION
	REMARKS

AMERICAN WOODCOCK *Scolopax minor*	DATE
	LOCATION
	REMARKS

WILSON'S PHALAROPE *Phalaropus tricolor*	DATE
	LOCATION
	REMARKS

RED-NECKED PHALAROPE *Phalaropus lobatus*	DATE
	LOCATION
	REMARKS

RED PHALAROPE *Phalaropus fulicaria*	DATE
	LOCATION
	REMARKS

	DATE
	LOCATION
	REMARKS

JAEGERS, SKUAS

POMARINE JAEGER

Stercorarius pomarinus

DATE

LOCATION

REMARKS

PARASITIC JAEGER

Stercorarius parasiticus

DATE

LOCATION

REMARKS

LONG-TAILED JAEGER

Stercorarius longicaudus

DATE

LOCATION

REMARKS

GREAT SKUA

Catharacta skua

DATE

LOCATION

REMARKS

SOUTH POLAR SKUA

Catharacta maccormicki

DATE

LOCATION

REMARKS

LAUGHING GULL *Larus atricilla*	DATE
	LOCATION
	REMARKS

FRANKLIN'S GULL *Larus pipixcan*	DATE
	LOCATION
	REMARKS

LITTLE GULL *Larus minutus*	DATE
	LOCATION
	REMARKS

COMMON BLACK-HEADED GULL *Larus ridibundus*	DATE
	LOCATION
	REMARKS

BONAPARTE'S GULL *Larus philadelphia*	DATE
	LOCATION
	REMARKS

60

GULLS

HEERMANN'S GULL *Larus heermanni*	DATE
	LOCATION
	REMARKS

MEW GULL *Larus canus*	DATE
	LOCATION
	REMARKS

RING-BILLED GULL *Larus delawarensis*	DATE
	LOCATION
	REMARKS

CALIFORNIA GULL *Larus californicus*	DATE
	LOCATION
	REMARKS

HERRING GULL *Larus argentatus*	DATE
	LOCATION
	REMARKS

THAYER'S GULL *Larus thayeri*	DATE
	LOCATION
	REMARKS

ICELAND GULL *Larus glaucoides*	DATE
	LOCATION
	REMARKS

LESSER BLACK-BACKED GULL *Larus fuscus*	DATE
	LOCATION
	REMARKS

YELLOW-FOOTED GULL *Larus livens*	DATE
	LOCATION
	REMARKS

WESTERN GULL *Larus occidentalis*	DATE
	LOCATION
	REMARKS

62

GULLS, KITTIWAKES

GLAUCOUS-WINGED GULL *Larus glaucescens*	DATE	
	LOCATION	
	REMARKS	

GLAUCOUS GULL *Larus hyperboreus*	DATE	
	LOCATION	
	REMARKS	

GREAT BLACK-BACKED GULL *Larus marinus*	DATE	
	LOCATION	
	REMARKS	

BLACK-LEGGED KITTIWAKE *Rissa tridactyla*	DATE	
	LOCATION	
	REMARKS	

RED-LEGGED KITTIWAKE *Rissa brevirostris*	DATE	
	LOCATION	
	REMARKS	

ROSS' GULL *Rhodostethia rosea*	DATE LOCATION REMARKS

SABINE'S GULL *Xema sabini*	DATE LOCATION REMARKS

IVORY GULL *Pagophila eburnea*	DATE LOCATION REMARKS

GULL-BILLED TERN *Sterna nilotica*	DATE LOCATION REMARKS

CASPIAN TERN *Sterna caspia*	DATE LOCATION REMARKS

64

TERNS

ROYAL TERN	DATE	
Sterna maxima	LOCATION	
	REMARKS	

ELEGANT TERN	DATE	
Sterna elegans	LOCATION	
	REMARKS	

SANDWICH TERN	DATE	
Sterna sandvicensis	LOCATION	
	REMARKS	

ROSEATE TERN	DATE	
Sterna dougallii	LOCATION	
	REMARKS	

COMMON TERN	DATE	
Sterna hirundo	LOCATION	
	REMARKS	

ARCTIC TERN *Sterna paradisaea*	DATE
	LOCATION
	REMARKS

FORSTER'S TERN *Sterna forsteri*	DATE
	LOCATION
	REMARKS

LEAST TERN *Sterna antillarum*	DATE
	LOCATION
	REMARKS

ALEUTIAN TERN *Sterna aleutica*	DATE
	LOCATION
	REMARKS

BRIDLED TERN *Sterna anaethetus*	DATE
	LOCATION
	REMARKS

TERNS, SKIMMER

SOOTY TERN *Sterna fuscata*	DATE
	LOCATION
	REMARKS

BLACK TERN *Chlidonias niger*	DATE
	LOCATION
	REMARKS

BROWN NODDY *Anous stolidus*	DATE
	LOCATION
	REMARKS

BLACK SKIMMER *Rynchops nigra*	DATE
	LOCATION
	REMARKS

	DATE
	LOCATION
	REMARKS

DOVEKIE

Alle alle

DATE	
LOCATION	
REMARKS	

COMMON MURRE

Uria aalge

DATE	
LOCATION	
REMARKS	

THICK-BILLED MURRE

Uria lomvia

DATE	
LOCATION	
REMARKS	

RAZORBILL

Alca torda

DATE	
LOCATION	
REMARKS	

BLACK GUILLEMOT

Cepphus grylle

DATE	
LOCATION	
REMARKS	

GUILLEMOT, MURRELETS

PIGEON GUILLEMOT

Cepphus columba

DATE	
LOCATION	
REMARKS	

MARBLED MURRELET

Brachyramphus marmoratus

DATE	
LOCATION	
REMARKS	

KITTLITZ'S MURRELET

Brachyramphus brevirostris

DATE	
LOCATION	
REMARKS	

XANTUS' MURRELET

Synthliboramphus hypoleucus

DATE	
LOCATION	
REMARKS	

CRAVERI'S MURRELET

Synthliboramphus craveri

DATE	
LOCATION	
REMARKS	

ANCIENT MURRELET

Synthliboramphus antiquus

DATE	
LOCATION	
REMARKS	

CASSIN'S AUKLET

Ptychoramphus aleuticus

DATE	
LOCATION	
REMARKS	

PARAKEET AUKLET

Cyclorrhynchus psittacula

DATE	
LOCATION	
REMARKS	

LEAST AUKLET

Aethia pusilla

DATE	
LOCATION	
REMARKS	

WHISKERED AUKLET

Aethia pygmaea

DATE	
LOCATION	
REMARKS	

70

AUKLETS, PUFFINS

CRESTED AUKLET
Aethia cristatella

DATE	
LOCATION	
REMARKS	

RHINOCEROS AUKLET
Cerorhinca monocerata

DATE	
LOCATION	
REMARKS	

TUFTED PUFFIN
Fratercula cirrhata

DATE	
LOCATION	
REMARKS	

ATLANTIC PUFFIN
Fratercula arctica

DATE	
LOCATION	
REMARKS	

HORNED PUFFIN
Fratercula corniculata

DATE	
LOCATION	
REMARKS	

DOVES, PIGEONS

ROCK DOVE *Columba livia*	DATE
	LOCATION
	REMARKS

WHITE- CROWNED PIGEON *Columba leucocephala*	DATE
	LOCATION
	REMARKS

RED-BILLED PIGEON *Columba flavirostris*	DATE
	LOCATION
	REMARKS

BAND-TAILED PIGEON *Columba fasciata*	DATE
	LOCATION
	REMARKS

EURASIAN COLLARED- DOVE *Streptopelia decaocto*	DATE
	LOCATION
	REMARKS

DOVES

	DATE	
RINGED TURTLE-DOVE *Streptopelia risoria*	LOCATION	
	REMARKS	

	DATE	
SPOTTED DOVE *Streptopelia chinensis*	LOCATION	
	REMARKS	

	DATE	
WHITE-WINGED DOVE *Zenaida asiatica*	LOCATION	
	REMARKS	

	DATE	
MOURNING DOVE *Zenaida macroura*	LOCATION	
	REMARKS	

	DATE	
INCA DOVE *Columbina inca*	LOCATION	
	REMARKS	

COMMON GROUND-DOVE *Columbina passerina*	DATE
	LOCATION
	REMARKS

WHITE-TIPPED DOVE *Leptotila verreauxi*	DATE
	LOCATION
	REMARKS

	DATE
	LOCATION
	REMARKS

	DATE
	LOCATION
	REMARKS

	DATE
	LOCATION
	REMARKS

PSITTACIFORMES

BUDGERIGAR, PARAKEETS, PARROT

BUDGERIGAR *Melopsittacus undulatus*	DATE
	LOCATION
	REMARKS

ROSE-RINGED PARAKEET *Psittacula krameri*	DATE
	LOCATION
	REMARKS

MONK PARAKEET *Myiopsitta monachus*	DATE
	LOCATION
	REMARKS

CANARY-WINGED PARAKEET *Brotogeris versicolurus*	DATE
	LOCATION
	REMARKS

RED-CROWNED PARROT *Amazona viridigenalis*	DATE
	LOCATION
	REMARKS

CUCKOOS, ROADRUNNER, ANI

	DATE	
BLACK-BILLED CUCKOO *Coccyzus erythropthalmus*	LOCATION	
	REMARKS	

	DATE	
YELLOW-BILLED CUCKOO *Coccyzus americanus*	LOCATION	
	REMARKS	

	DATE	
MANGROVE CUCKOO *Coccyzus minor*	LOCATION	
	REMARKS	

	DATE	
GREATER ROADRUNNER *Geococcyx californianus*	LOCATION	
	REMARKS	

	DATE	
SMOOTH-BILLED ANI *Crotophaga ani*	LOCATION	
	REMARKS	

76

ANI

GROOVE-BILLED ANI *Crotophaga sulcirostris*	DATE
	LOCATION
	REMARKS

	DATE
	LOCATION
	REMARKS

	DATE
	LOCATION
	REMARKS

	DATE
	LOCATION
	REMARKS

	DATE
	LOCATION
	REMARKS

BARN OWL

Tyto alba

DATE
LOCATION

REMARKS

FLAMMULATED OWL

Otus flammeolus

DATE
LOCATION

REMARKS

EASTERN SCREECH-OWL

Otus asio

DATE
LOCATION

REMARKS

WESTERN SCREECH-OWL

Otus kennicottii

DATE
LOCATION

REMARKS

WHISKERED SCREECH-OWL

Otus trichopsis

DATE
LOCATION

REMARKS

78

OWLS

GREAT HORNED OWL *Bubo virginianus*	DATE
	LOCATION
	REMARKS

SNOWY OWL *Nyctea scandiaca*	DATE
	LOCATION
	REMARKS

NORTHERN HAWK OWL *Surnia ulula*	DATE
	LOCATION
	REMARKS

NORTHERN PYGMY-OWL *Glaucidium gnoma*	DATE
	LOCATION
	REMARKS

FERRUGINOUS PYGMY-OWL *Glaucidium brasilianum*	DATE
	LOCATION
	REMARKS

ELF OWL

Micrathene whitneyi

DATE	
LOCATION	
REMARKS	

BURROWING OWL

Athene cunicularia

DATE	
LOCATION	
REMARKS	

SPOTTED OWL

Strix occidentalis

DATE	
LOCATION	
REMARKS	

BARRED OWL

Strix varia

DATE	
LOCATION	
REMARKS	

GREAT GRAY OWL

Strix nebulosa

DATE	
LOCATION	
REMARKS	

80

OWLS

LONG-EARED OWL *Asio otus*	DATE
	LOCATION
	REMARKS

SHORT-EARED OWL *Asio flammeus*	DATE
	LOCATION
	REMARKS

BOREAL OWL *Aegolius funereus*	DATE
	LOCATION
	REMARKS

NORTHERN SAW-WHET OWL *Aegolius acadicus*	DATE
	LOCATION
	REMARKS

	DATE
	LOCATION
	REMARKS

NIGHTHAWKS, GOATSUCKERS

LESSER NIGHTHAWK *Chordeiles acutipennis*	DATE
	LOCATION
	REMARKS

COMMON NIGHTHAWK *Chordeiles minor*	DATE
	LOCATION
	REMARKS

ANTILLEAN NIGHTHAWK *Chordeiles gundlachii*	DATE
	LOCATION
	REMARKS

PAURAQUE *Nyctidromus albicollis*	DATE
	LOCATION
	REMARKS

COMMON POORWILL *Phalaenoptilus nuttallii*	DATE
	LOCATION
	REMARKS

82

GOATSUCKERS

CHUCK-WILL'S-WIDOW

Caprimulgus carolinensis

DATE	
LOCATION	
REMARKS	

BUFF-COLLARED NIGHTJAR

Caprimulgus ridgwayi

DATE	
LOCATION	
REMARKS	

WHIP-POOR-WILL

Caprimulgus vociferus

DATE	
LOCATION	
REMARKS	

DATE	
LOCATION	
REMARKS	

DATE	
LOCATION	
REMARKS	

BLACK SWIFT

Cypseloides niger

DATE	
LOCATION	
REMARKS	

CHIMNEY SWIFT

Chaetura pelagica

DATE	
LOCATION	
REMARKS	

VAUX'S SWIFT

Chaetura vauxi

DATE	
LOCATION	
REMARKS	

WHITE-THROATED SWIFT

Aeronautes saxatalis

DATE	
LOCATION	
REMARKS	

BROAD-BILLED HUMMINGBIRD

Cynanthus latirostris

DATE	
LOCATION	
REMARKS	

HUMMINGBIRDS

WHITE-EARED HUMMINGBIRD

Hylocharis leucotis

DATE	
LOCATION	
REMARKS	

BERYLLINE HUMMINGBIRD

Amazilia beryllina

DATE	
LOCATION	
REMARKS	

BUFF-BELLIED HUMMINGBIRD

Amazilia yucatanensis

DATE	
LOCATION	
REMARKS	

VIOLET-CROWNED HUMMINGBIRD

Amazilia violiceps

DATE	
LOCATION	
REMARKS	

BLUE-THROATED HUMMINGBIRD

Lampornis clemenciae

DATE	
LOCATION	
REMARKS	

MAGNIFICENT HUMMINGBIRD

Eugenes fulgens

DATE	
LOCATION	
REMARKS	

LUCIFER HUMMINGBIRD

Calothorax lucifer

DATE	
LOCATION	
REMARKS	

RUBY- THROATED HUMMINGBIRD

Archilochus colubris

DATE	
LOCATION	
REMARKS	

BLACK- CHINNED HUMMINGBIRD

Archilochus alexandri

DATE	
LOCATION	
REMARKS	

ANNA'S HUMMINGBIRD

Calypte anna

DATE	
LOCATION	
REMARKS	

HUMMINGBIRDS

COSTA'S HUMMINGBIRD

Calypte costae

DATE	
LOCATION	
REMARKS	

CALLIOPE HUMMINGBIRD

Stellula calliope

DATE	
LOCATION	
REMARKS	

BROAD-TAILED HUMMINGBIRD

Selasphorus platycercus

DATE	
LOCATION	
REMARKS	

RUFOUS HUMMINGBIRD

Selasphorus rufus

DATE	
LOCATION	
REMARKS	

ALLEN'S HUMMINGBIRD

Selasphorus sasin

DATE	
LOCATION	
REMARKS	

ELEGANT TROGON	DATE
	LOCATION
Trogon elegans	REMARKS

	DATE
	LOCATION
	REMARKS

	DATE
	LOCATION
	REMARKS

	DATE
	LOCATION
	REMARKS

	DATE
	LOCATION
	REMARKS

CORACIIFORMES

KINGFISHERS

RINGED KINGFISHER *Ceryle torquata*	DATE
	LOCATION
	REMARKS

BELTED KINGFISHER *Ceryle alcyon*	DATE
	LOCATION
	REMARKS

GREEN KINGFISHER *Chloroceryle americana*	DATE
	LOCATION
	REMARKS

	DATE
	LOCATION
	REMARKS

	DATE
	LOCATION
	REMARKS

PICIFORMES

WOODPECKERS

LEWIS' WOODPECKER

Melanerpes lewis

DATE
LOCATION

REMARKS

RED-HEADED WOODPECKER

Melanerpes erythrocephalus

DATE
LOCATION

REMARKS

ACORN WOODPECKER

Melanerpes formicivorus

DATE
LOCATION

REMARKS

GILA WOODPECKER

Centurus uropygialis

DATE
LOCATION

REMARKS

GOLDEN-FRONTED WOODPECKER

Melanerpes aurifrons

DATE
LOCATION

REMARKS

WOODPECKER, SAPSUCKERS

RED-BELLIED WOODPECKER Melanerpes carolinus	DATE
	LOCATION
	REMARKS

YELLOW-BELLIED SAPSUCKER Sphyrapicus varius	DATE
	LOCATION
	REMARKS

RED-NAPED SAPSUCKER Sphyrapicus nuchalis	DATE
	LOCATION
	REMARKS

RED-BREASTED SAPSUCKER Sphyrapicus ruber	DATE
	LOCATION
	REMARKS

WILLIAMSON'S SAPSUCKER Sphyrapicus thyroideus	DATE
	LOCATION
	REMARKS

**LADDER-
BACKED
WOODPECKER**

Picoides scalaris

DATE	
LOCATION	
REMARKS	

**NUTTALL'S
WOODPECKER**

Picoides nuttallii

DATE	
LOCATION	
REMARKS	

**DOWNY
WOODPECKER**

Picoides pubescens

DATE	
LOCATION	
REMARKS	

**HAIRY
WOODPECKER**

Picoides villosus

DATE	
LOCATION	
REMARKS	

**STRICKLAND'S
WOODPECKER**

Picoides stricklandi

DATE	
LOCATION	
REMARKS	

WOODPECKERS, FLICKER

RED-COCKADED WOODPECKER *Picoides borealis*	DATE
	LOCATION
	REMARKS

WHITE-HEADED WOODPECKER *Picoides albolarvatus*	DATE
	LOCATION
	REMARKS

THREE-TOED WOODPECKER *Picoides tridactylus*	DATE
	LOCATION
	REMARKS

BLACK-BACKED WOODPECKER *Picoides arcticus*	DATE
	LOCATION
	REMARKS

NORTHERN FLICKER "YELLOW-SHAFTED" *Colaptes auratus*	DATE
	LOCATION
	REMARKS

"RED-SHAFTED" FLICKER *(subspecies of Northern Flicker)*	DATE
	LOCATION
	REMARKS

"GILDED" FLICKER *(subspecies of Northern Flicker)*	DATE
	LOCATION
	REMARKS

PILEATED WOODPECKER *Dryocopus pileatus*	DATE
	LOCATION
	REMARKS

	DATE
	LOCATION
	REMARKS

	DATE
	LOCATION
	REMARKS

PASSERIFORMES

FLYCATCHERS, WOOD-PEWEES

NORTHERN BEARDLESS-TYRANNULET *Camptostoma imberbe*	DATE LOCATION REMARKS

OLIVE-SIDED FLYCATCHER *Contopus borealis*	DATE LOCATION REMARKS

GREATER PEWEE *Contopus pertinax*	DATE LOCATION REMARKS

WESTERN WOOD-PEWEE *Contopus sordidulus*	DATE LOCATION REMARKS

EASTERN WOOD-PEWEE *Contopus virens*	DATE LOCATION REMARKS

YELLOW-BELLIED FLYCATCHER

Empidonax flaviventris

DATE
LOCATION
REMARKS

ACADIAN FLYCATCHER

Empidonax virescens

DATE
LOCATION
REMARKS

ALDER FLYCATCHER

Empidonax alnorum

DATE
LOCATION
REMARKS

WILLOW FLYCATCHER

Empidonax traillii

DATE
LOCATION
REMARKS

LEAST FLYCATCHER

Empidonax minimus

DATE
LOCATION
REMARKS

EMPIDONAX FLYCATCHERS

HAMMOND'S FLYCATCHER

Empidonax hammondii

DATE

LOCATION

REMARKS

DUSKY FLYCATCHER

Empidonax oberholseri

DATE

LOCATION

REMARKS

GRAY FLYCATCHER

Empidonax wrightii

DATE

LOCATION

REMARKS

PACIFIC-SLOPE FLYCATCHER

Empidonax difficilis

DATE

LOCATION

REMARKS

CORDILLERAN FLYCATCHER

Empidonax occidentalis

DATE

LOCATION

REMARKS

BUFF-BREASTED FLYCATCHER *Empidonax fulvifrons*	DATE
	LOCATION
	REMARKS

BLACK PHOEBE *Sayornis nigricans*	DATE
	LOCATION
	REMARKS

EASTERN PHOEBE *Sayornis phoebe*	DATE
	LOCATION
	REMARKS

SAY'S PHOEBE *Sayornis saya*	DATE
	LOCATION
	REMARKS

VERMILION FLYCATCHER *Pyrocephalus rubinus*	DATE
	LOCATION
	REMARKS

98

FLYCATCHERS

DUSKY-CAPPED FLYCATCHER *Myiarchus tuberculifer*	DATE
	LOCATION
	REMARKS

ASH-THROATED FLYCATCHER *Myiarchus cinerascens*	DATE
	LOCATION
	REMARKS

GREAT CRESTED FLYCATCHER *Myiarchus crinitus*	DATE
	LOCATION
	REMARKS

BROWN-CRESTED FLYCATCHER *Myiarchus tyrannulus*	DATE
	LOCATION
	REMARKS

GREAT KISKADEE *Pitangus sulphuratus*	DATE
	LOCATION
	REMARKS

SULPHUR-BELLIED FLYCATCHER *Myiodynastes luteiventris*	DATE
	LOCATION
	REMARKS

TROPICAL KINGBIRD *Tyrannus melancholicus*	DATE
	LOCATION
	REMARKS

COUCH'S KINGBIRD *Tyrannus couchii*	DATE
	LOCATION
	REMARKS

CASSIN'S KINGBIRD *Tyrannus vociferans*	DATE
	LOCATION
	REMARKS

THICK-BILLED KINGBIRD *Tyrannus crassirostris*	DATE
	LOCATION
	REMARKS

KINGBIRDS, FLYCATCHERS

WESTERN KINGBIRD *Tyrannus verticalis*	DATE
	LOCATION
	REMARKS

EASTERN KINGBIRD *Tyrannus tyrannus*	DATE
	LOCATION
	REMARKS

GRAY KINGBIRD *Tyrannus dominicensis*	DATE
	LOCATION
	REMARKS

SCISSOR-TAILED FLYCATCHER *Tyrannus forficatus*	DATE
	LOCATION
	REMARKS

FORK-TAILED FLYCATCHER *Tyrannus savana*	DATE
	LOCATION
	REMARKS

ROSE-THROATED BECARD

Pachyramphus aglaiae

DATE	
LOCATION	
REMARKS	

EURASIAN SKYLARK

Alauda arvensis

DATE	
LOCATION	
REMARKS	

HORNED LARK

Eremophila alpestris

DATE	
LOCATION	
REMARKS	

DATE	
LOCATION	
REMARKS	

DATE	
LOCATION	
REMARKS	

102

MARTIN, SWALLOWS

PURPLE MARTIN *Progne subis*	DATE	
	LOCATION	
	REMARKS	

TREE SWALLOW *Tachycineta bicolor*	DATE	
	LOCATION	
	REMARKS	

VIOLET-GREEN SWALLOW *Tachycineta thalassina*	DATE	
	LOCATION	
	REMARKS	

BAHAMA SWALLOW *Tachycineta cyaneoviridis*	DATE	
	LOCATION	
	REMARKS	

NORTHERN ROUGH-WINGED SWALLOW *Stelgidopteryx serripennis*	DATE	
	LOCATION	
	REMARKS	

BANK SWALLOW	DATE
Riparia riparia	LOCATION
	REMARKS

CLIFF SWALLOW	DATE
Hirundo pyrrhonota	LOCATION
	REMARKS

CAVE SWALLOW	DATE
Hirundo fulva	LOCATION
	REMARKS

BARN SWALLOW	DATE
Hirundo rustica	LOCATION
	REMARKS

	DATE
	LOCATION
	REMARKS

104

JAYS

GRAY JAY
Perisoreus canadensis

DATE

LOCATION

REMARKS

STELLER'S JAY
Cyanocitta stelleri

DATE

LOCATION

REMARKS

BLUE JAY
Cyanocitta cristata

DATE

LOCATION

REMARKS

GREEN JAY
Cyanocorax yncas

DATE

LOCATION

REMARKS

BROWN JAY
Cyanocorax morio

DATE

LOCATION

REMARKS

SCRUB JAY *Aphelocoma coerulescens*	DATE
	LOCATION
	REMARKS

GRAY-BREASTED JAY *Aphelocoma ultramarina*	DATE
	LOCATION
	REMARKS

PINYON JAY *Gymnorhinus cyanocephalus*	DATE
	LOCATION
	REMARKS

CLARK'S NUTCRACKER *Nucifraga columbiana*	DATE
	LOCATION
	REMARKS

BLACK-BILLED MAGPIE *Pica pica*	DATE
	LOCATION
	REMARKS

MAGPIE, CROWS

YELLOW-BILLED MAGPIE *Pica nuttalli*	DATE
	LOCATION
	REMARKS

EURASIAN JACKDAW *Corvus monedula*	DATE
	LOCATION
	REMARKS

AMERICAN CROW *Corvus brachyrhynchos*	DATE
	LOCATION
	REMARKS

NORTHWESTERN CROW *Corvus caurinus*	DATE
	LOCATION
	REMARKS

MEXICAN CROW *Corvus imparatus*	DATE
	LOCATION
	REMARKS

FISH CROW

Corvus ossifragus

DATE
LOCATION

REMARKS

CHIHUAHUAN RAVEN

Corvus cryptoleucus

DATE
LOCATION

REMARKS

COMMON RAVEN

Corvus corax

DATE
LOCATION

REMARKS

DATE
LOCATION

REMARKS

DATE
LOCATION

REMARKS

CHICKADEES

BLACK-CAPPED CHICKADEE *Parus atricapillus*	DATE
	LOCATION
	REMARKS

CAROLINA CHICKADEE *Parus carolinensis*	DATE
	LOCATION
	REMARKS

MEXICAN CHICKADEE *Parus sclateri*	DATE
	LOCATION
	REMARKS

MOUNTAIN CHICKADEE *Parus gambeli*	DATE
	LOCATION
	REMARKS

SIBERIAN TIT *Parus cinctus*	DATE
	LOCATION
	REMARKS

BOREAL CHICKADEE *Parus hudsonicus*	DATE
	LOCATION
	REMARKS

CHESTNUT-BACKED CHICKADEE *Parus rufescens*	DATE
	LOCATION
	REMARKS

BRIDLED TITMOUSE *Parus wollweberi*	DATE
	LOCATION
	REMARKS

PLAIN TITMOUSE *Parus inornatus*	DATE
	LOCATION
	REMARKS

TUFTED TITMOUSE *Parus bicolor*	DATE
	LOCATION
	REMARKS

TITMOUSE, VERDIN, BUSHTIT, NUTHATCH

"BLACK-CRESTED" TITMOUSE *(subspecies of Tufted Titmouse)*	DATE
	LOCATION
	REMARKS

VERDIN *Auriparus flaviceps*	DATE
	LOCATION
	REMARKS

BUSHTIT *Psaltriparus minimus*	DATE
	LOCATION
	REMARKS

"BLACK-EARED" BUSHTIT *(color morph of Bushtit)*	DATE
	LOCATION
	REMARKS

RED-BREASTED NUTHATCH *Sitta canadensis*	DATE
	LOCATION
	REMARKS

WHITE-BREASTED NUTHATCH *Sitta carolinensis*	DATE
	LOCATION
	REMARKS

PYGMY NUTHATCH *Sitta pygmaea*	DATE
	LOCATION
	REMARKS

BROWN-HEADED NUTHATCH *Sitta pusilla*	DATE
	LOCATION
	REMARKS

BROWN CREEPER *Certhia americana*	DATE
	LOCATION
	REMARKS

RED-WHISKERED BULBUL *Pycnonotus jocosus*	DATE
	LOCATION
	REMARKS

112

WRENS

CACTUS WREN *Campylorhynchus brunneicapillus*	DATE
	LOCATION
	REMARKS

ROCK WREN *Salpinctes obsoletus*	DATE
	LOCATION
	REMARKS

CANYON WREN *Catherpes mexicanus*	DATE
	LOCATION
	REMARKS

CAROLINA WREN *Thryothorus ludovicianus*	DATE
	LOCATION
	REMARKS

BEWICK'S WREN *Thryomanes bewickii*	DATE
	LOCATION
	REMARKS

	DATE
HOUSE WREN	LOCATION
Troglodytes aedon	REMARKS

	DATE
"BROWN-THROATED" WREN	LOCATION
(subspecies of House Wren)	REMARKS

	DATE
WINTER WREN	LOCATION
Troglodytes troglodytes	REMARKS

	DATE
SEDGE WREN	LOCATION
Cistothorus platensis	REMARKS

	DATE
MARSH WREN	LOCATION
Cistothorus palustris	REMARKS

114

DIPPER, KINGLETS

AMERICAN DIPPER *Cinclus mexicanus*	DATE
	LOCATION
	REMARKS

ARCTIC WARBLER *Phylloscopus borealis*	DATE
	LOCATION
	REMARKS

GOLDEN-CROWNED KINGLET *Regulus satrapa*	DATE
	LOCATION
	REMARKS

RUBY-CROWNED KINGLET *Regulus calendula*	DATE
	LOCATION
	REMARKS

	DATE
	LOCATION
	REMARKS

BLUE-GRAY GNATCATCHER *Polioptila caerulea*	DATE
	LOCATION
	REMARKS

CALIFORNIA GNATCATCHER *Polioptila californica*	DATE
	LOCATION
	REMARKS

BLACK-TAILED GNATCATCHER *Polioptila melanura*	DATE
	LOCATION
	REMARKS

BLACK-CAPPED GNATCATCHER *Polioptila nigriceps*	DATE
	LOCATION
	REMARKS

BLUETHROAT *Luscinia svecica*	DATE
	LOCATION
	REMARKS

116

WHEATEAR, BLUEBIRDS, SOLITAIRE

NORTHERN WHEATEAR
Oenanthe oenanthe

DATE
LOCATION
REMARKS

EASTERN BLUEBIRD
Sialia sialis

DATE
LOCATION
REMARKS

WESTERN BLUEBIRD
Sialia mexicana

DATE
LOCATION
REMARKS

MOUNTAIN BLUEBIRD
Sialia currucoides

DATE
LOCATION
REMARKS

TOWNSEND'S SOLITAIRE
Myadestes townsendi

DATE
LOCATION
REMARKS

	DATE
VEERY	LOCATION
Catharus fuscescens	REMARKS

	DATE
GRAY-CHEEKED THRUSH	LOCATION
Catharus minimus	REMARKS

	DATE
SWAINSON'S THRUSH	LOCATION
Catharus ustulatus	REMARKS

	DATE
HERMIT THRUSH	LOCATION
Catharus guttatus	REMARKS

	DATE
WOOD THRUSH	LOCATION
Hylocichla mustelina	REMARKS

ROBINS, WRENTIT

CLAY-COLORED ROBIN *Turdus grayi*	DATE
	LOCATION
	REMARKS

RUFOUS-BACKED ROBIN *Turdus rufopalliatus*	DATE
	LOCATION
	REMARKS

AMERICAN ROBIN *Turdus migratorius*	DATE
	LOCATION
	REMARKS

VARIED THRUSH *Ixoreus naevius*	DATE
	LOCATION
	REMARKS

WRENTIT *Chamaea fasciata*	DATE
	LOCATION
	REMARKS

GRAY CATBIRD

Dumetella carolinensis

DATE
LOCATION
REMARKS

NORTHERN MOCKINGBIRD

Mimus polyglottos

DATE
LOCATION
REMARKS

SAGE THRASHER

Oreoscoptes montanus

DATE
LOCATION
REMARKS

BROWN THRASHER

Toxostoma rufum

DATE
LOCATION
REMARKS

LONG-BILLED THRASHER

Toxostoma longirostre

DATE
LOCATION
REMARKS

120

THRASHERS

BENDIRE'S THRASHER *Toxostoma bendirei*	DATE
	LOCATION
	REMARKS

CURVE-BILLED THRASHER *Toxostoma curvirostre*	DATE
	LOCATION
	REMARKS

CALIFORNIA THRASHER *Toxostoma redivivum*	DATE
	LOCATION
	REMARKS

CRISSAL THRASHER *Toxostoma crissale*	DATE
	LOCATION
	REMARKS

LE CONTE'S THRASHER *Toxostoma lecontei*	DATE
	LOCATION
	REMARKS

YELLOW WAGTAIL
Motacilla flava

DATE
LOCATION
REMARKS

WHITE WAGTAIL
Motacilla alba

DATE
LOCATION
REMARKS

RED-THROATED PIPIT
Anthus cervinus

DATE
LOCATION
REMARKS

AMERICAN PIPIT
Anthus rubescens

DATE
LOCATION
REMARKS

SPRAGUE'S PIPIT
Anthus spragueii

DATE
LOCATION
REMARKS

WAXWINGS, PHAINOPEPLA

BOHEMIAN WAXWING *Bombycilla garrulus*	DATE
	LOCATION
	REMARKS

CEDAR WAXWING *Bombycilla cedrorum*	DATE
	LOCATION
	REMARKS

PHAINOPEPLA *Phainopepla nitens*	DATE
	LOCATION
	REMARKS

	DATE
	LOCATION
	REMARKS

	DATE
	LOCATION
	REMARKS

NORTHERN SHRIKE	DATE	
Lanius excubitor	LOCATION	
	REMARKS	

LOGGERHEAD SHRIKE	DATE	
Lanius ludovicianus	LOCATION	
	REMARKS	

EUROPEAN STARLING	DATE	
Sturnus vulgaris	LOCATION	
	REMARKS	

CRESTED MYNA	DATE	
Acridotheres cristatellus	LOCATION	
	REMARKS	

	DATE	
	LOCATION	
	REMARKS	

124

VIREOS

WHITE-EYED VIREO *Vireo griseus*	DATE
	LOCATION
	REMARKS

BELL'S VIREO *Vireo bellii*	DATE
	LOCATION
	REMARKS

BLACK-CAPPED VIREO *Vireo atricapillus*	DATE
	LOCATION
	REMARKS

GRAY VIREO *Vireo vicinior*	DATE
	LOCATION
	REMARKS

SOLITARY VIREO *Vireo solitarius*	DATE
	LOCATION
	REMARKS

YELLOW-THROATED VIREO

Vireo flavifrons

DATE	
LOCATION	
REMARKS	

HUTTON'S VIREO

Vireo huttoni

DATE	
LOCATION	
REMARKS	

WARBLING VIREO

Vireo gilvus

DATE	
LOCATION	
REMARKS	

PHILADELPHIA VIREO

Vireo philadelphicus

DATE	
LOCATION	
REMARKS	

RED-EYED VIREO

Vireo olivaceus

DATE	
LOCATION	
REMARKS	

VIREOS

YELLOW-GREEN VIREO *Vireo flavoviridis*	DATE LOCATION REMARKS

BLACK-WHISKERED VIREO *Vireo altiloquus*	DATE LOCATION REMARKS

	DATE LOCATION REMARKS

	DATE LOCATION REMARKS

	DATE LOCATION REMARKS

BLUE-WINGED WARBLER

Vermivora pinus

DATE	
LOCATION	
REMARKS	

GOLDEN-WINGED WARBLER

Vermivora chrysoptera

DATE	
LOCATION	
REMARKS	

"BREWSTER'S" WARBLER

(hybrid between Blue-winged and Golden-winged Warblers)

DATE	
LOCATION	
REMARKS	

"LAWRENCE'S" WARBLER

(hybrid between Blue-winged and Golden-winged Warblers)

DATE	
LOCATION	
REMARKS	

TENNESSEE WARBLER

Vermivora peregrina

DATE	
LOCATION	
REMARKS	

128

WARBLERS

ORANGE-CROWNED WARBLER *Vermivora celata*	DATE
	LOCATION
	REMARKS

NASHVILLE WARBLER *Vermivora ruficapilla*	DATE
	LOCATION
	REMARKS

VIRGINIA'S WARBLER *Vermivora virginiae*	DATE
	LOCATION
	REMARKS

COLIMA WARBLER *Vermivora crissalis*	DATE
	LOCATION
	REMARKS

LUCY'S WARBLER *Vermivora luciae*	DATE
	LOCATION
	REMARKS

NORTHERN PARULA

Parula americana

| DATE |
| LOCATION |
| REMARKS |

TROPICAL PARULA

Parula pitiayumi

| DATE |
| LOCATION |
| REMARKS |

YELLOW WARBLER

Dendroica petechia

| DATE |
| LOCATION |
| REMARKS |

CHESTNUT-SIDED WARBLER

Dendroica pensylvanica

| DATE |
| LOCATION |
| REMARKS |

MAGNOLIA WARBLER

Dendroica magnolia

| DATE |
| LOCATION |
| REMARKS |

130

WARBLERS

	DATE
CAPE MAY WARBLER *Dendroica tigrina*	LOCATION
	REMARKS

	DATE
BLACK-THROATED BLUE WARBLER *Dendroica caerulescens*	LOCATION
	REMARKS

	DATE
YELLOW-RUMPED WARBLER "MYRTLE" *Dendroica coronata*	LOCATION
	REMARKS

	DATE
"AUDUBON'S" WARBLER *(subspecies of Yellow-rumped Warbler)*	LOCATION
	REMARKS

	DATE
BLACK-THROATED GRAY WARBLER *Dendroica nigrescens*	LOCATION
	REMARKS

TOWNSEND'S WARBLER

Dendroica townsendi

DATE

LOCATION

REMARKS

HERMIT WARBLER

Dendroica occidentalis

DATE

LOCATION

REMARKS

BLACK-THROATED GREEN WARBLER

Dendroica virens

DATE

LOCATION

REMARKS

GOLDEN-CHEEKED WARBLER

Dendroica chrysoparia

DATE

LOCATION

REMARKS

BLACKBURNIAN WARBLER

Dendroica fusca

DATE

LOCATION

REMARKS

WARBLERS

	DATE
YELLOW-THROATED WARBLER *Dendroica dominica*	LOCATION
	REMARKS

	DATE
GRACE'S WARBLER *Dendroica graciae*	LOCATION
	REMARKS

	DATE
PINE WARBLER *Dendroica pinus*	LOCATION
	REMARKS

	DATE
KIRTLAND'S WARBLER *Dendroica kirtlandii*	LOCATION
	REMARKS

	DATE
PRAIRIE WARBLER *Dendroica discolor*	LOCATION
	REMARKS

PALM WARBLER

Dendroica palmarum

DATE

LOCATION

REMARKS

BAY-BREASTED WARBLER

Dendroica castanea

DATE

LOCATION

REMARKS

BLACKPOLL WARBLER

Dendroica striata

DATE

LOCATION

REMARKS

CERULEAN WARBLER

Dendroica cerulea

DATE

LOCATION

REMARKS

BLACK-AND-WHITE WARBLER

Mniotilta varia

DATE

LOCATION

REMARKS

134

REDSTART, WARBLERS, OVENBIRD

AMERICAN REDSTART

Setophaga ruticilla

DATE	
LOCATION	
REMARKS	

PROTHONOTARY WARBLER

Protonotaria citrea

DATE	
LOCATION	
REMARKS	

WORM-EATING WARBLER

Helmitheros vermivorus

DATE	
LOCATION	
REMARKS	

SWAINSON'S WARBLER

Limnothlypis swainsonii

DATE	
LOCATION	
REMARKS	

OVENBIRD

Seiurus aurocapillus

DATE	
LOCATION	
REMARKS	

NORTHERN WATERTHRUSH *Seiurus noveboracensis*	DATE
	LOCATION
	REMARKS

LOUISIANA WATERTHRUSH *Seiurus motacilla*	DATE
	LOCATION
	REMARKS

KENTUCKY WARBLER *Oporornis formosus*	DATE
	LOCATION
	REMARKS

CONNECTICUT WARBLER *Oporornis agilis*	DATE
	LOCATION
	REMARKS

MOURNING WARBLER *Oporornis philadelphia*	DATE
	LOCATION
	REMARKS

YELLOWTHROAT, WARBLERS

MacGILLIVRAY'S WARBLER *Oporornis tolmiei*	DATE
	LOCATION
	REMARKS

COMMON YELLOWTHROAT *Geothlypis trichas*	DATE
	LOCATION
	REMARKS

HOODED WARBLER *Wilsonia citrina*	DATE
	LOCATION
	REMARKS

WILSON'S WARBLER *Wilsonia pusilla*	DATE
	LOCATION
	REMARKS

CANADA WARBLER *Wilsonia canadensis*	DATE
	LOCATION
	REMARKS

RED-FACED WARBLER

Cardellina rubrifrons

DATE	
LOCATION	
REMARKS	

PAINTED REDSTART

Myioborus pictus

DATE	
LOCATION	
REMARKS	

RUFOUS-CAPPED WARBLER

Basileuterus rufifrons

DATE	
LOCATION	
REMARKS	

YELLOW-BREASTED CHAT

Icteria virens

DATE	
LOCATION	
REMARKS	

OLIVE WARBLER

Peucedramus taeniatus

DATE	
LOCATION	
REMARKS	

BANANAQUIT

BANANAQUIT *Coereba flaveola*	DATE
	LOCATION
	REMARKS

	DATE
	LOCATION
	REMARKS

	DATE
	LOCATION
	REMARKS

	DATE
	LOCATION
	REMARKS

	DATE
	LOCATION
	REMARKS

STRIPE-HEADED TANAGER *Spindalis zena*	DATE
	LOCATION
	REMARKS

HEPATIC TANAGER *Piranga flava*	DATE
	LOCATION
	REMARKS

SUMMER TANAGER *Piranga rubra*	DATE
	LOCATION
	REMARKS

SCARLET TANAGER *Piranga olivacea*	DATE
	LOCATION
	REMARKS

WESTERN TANAGER *Piranga ludoviciana*	DATE
	LOCATION
	REMARKS

CARDINALS, GROSBEAKS

NORTHERN CARDINAL *Cardinalis cardinalis*	DATE	
	LOCATION	
	REMARKS	

PYRRHULOXIA *Cardinalis sinuatus*	DATE	
	LOCATION	
	REMARKS	

ROSE-BREASTED GROSBEAK *Pheucticus ludovicianus*	DATE	
	LOCATION	
	REMARKS	

BLACK-HEADED GROSBEAK *Pheucticus melanocephalus*	DATE	
	LOCATION	
	REMARKS	

BLUE GROSBEAK *Guiraca caerulea*	DATE	
	LOCATION	
	REMARKS	

LAZULI BUNTING *Passerina amoena*	DATE
	LOCATION
	REMARKS

INDIGO BUNTING *Passerina cyanea*	DATE
	LOCATION
	REMARKS

VARIED BUNTING *Passerina versicolor*	DATE
	LOCATION
	REMARKS

PAINTED BUNTING *Passerina ciris*	DATE
	LOCATION
	REMARKS

DICKCISSEL *Spiza americana*	DATE
	LOCATION
	REMARKS

142

SPARROW, TOWHEES

OLIVE SPARROW

Arremonops rufivirgatus

DATE	
LOCATION	
REMARKS	

GREEN-TAILED TOWHEE

Pipilo chlorurus

DATE	
LOCATION	
REMARKS	

RUFOUS-SIDED TOWHEE

Pipilo erythrophthalmus

DATE	
LOCATION	
REMARKS	

CALIFORNIA TOWHEE

Pipilo crissalis

DATE	
LOCATION	
REMARKS	

CANYON TOWHEE

Pipilo fuscus

DATE	
LOCATION	
REMARKS	

ABERT'S TOWHEE *Pipilo aberti*	DATE LOCATION REMARKS

WHITE-COLLARED SEEDEATER *Sporophila torqueola*	DATE LOCATION REMARKS

BACHMAN'S SPARROW *Aimophila aestivalis*	DATE LOCATION REMARKS

BOTTERI'S SPARROW *Aimophila botterii*	DATE LOCATION REMARKS

CASSIN'S SPARROW *Aimophila cassinii*	DATE LOCATION REMARKS

144

SPARROWS

RUFOUS-WINGED SPARROW *Aimophila carpalis*	DATE
	LOCATION
	REMARKS

RUFOUS-CROWNED SPARROW *Aimophila ruficeps*	DATE
	LOCATION
	REMARKS

AMERICAN TREE SPARROW *Spizella arborea*	DATE
	LOCATION
	REMARKS

CHIPPING SPARROW *Spizella passerina*	DATE
	LOCATION
	REMARKS

CLAY-COLORED SPARROW *Spizella pallida*	DATE
	LOCATION
	REMARKS

BREWER'S SPARROW

Spizella breweri

DATE

LOCATION

REMARKS

FIELD SPARROW

Spizella pusilla

DATE

LOCATION

REMARKS

BLACK-CHINNED SPARROW

Spizella atrogularis

DATE

LOCATION

REMARKS

VESPER SPARROW

Pooecetes gramineus

DATE

LOCATION

REMARKS

LARK SPARROW

Chondestes grammacus

DATE

LOCATION

REMARKS

SPARROWS, BUNTING

BLACK-THROATED SPARROW *Amphispiza bilineata*	DATE
	LOCATION
	REMARKS

SAGE SPARROW *Amphispiza belli*	DATE
	LOCATION
	REMARKS

FIVE-STRIPED SPARROW *Amphispiza quinquestriata*	DATE
	LOCATION
	REMARKS

LARK BUNTING *Calamospiza melanocorys*	DATE
	LOCATION
	REMARKS

SAVANNAH SPARROW *Passerculus sandwichensis*	DATE
	LOCATION
	REMARKS

"IPSWICH" SPARROW *(subspecies of Savannah Sparrow)*	DATE
	LOCATION
	REMARKS

BAIRD'S SPARROW *Ammodramus bairdii*	DATE
	LOCATION
	REMARKS

GRASSHOPPER SPARROW *Ammodramus savannarum*	DATE
	LOCATION
	REMARKS

HENSLOW'S SPARROW *Ammodramus henslowii*	DATE
	LOCATION
	REMARKS

LE CONTE'S SPARROW *Ammodramus leconteii*	DATE
	LOCATION
	REMARKS

148

SPARROWS

SHARP-TAILED SPARROW

Ammodramus caudacutus

DATE	
LOCATION	
REMARKS	

SEASIDE SPARROW

Ammodramus maritimus

DATE	
LOCATION	
REMARKS	

"CAPE SABLE" SEASIDE-SPARROW

(subspecies of Seaside Sparrow)

DATE	
LOCATION	
REMARKS	

"DUSKY" SEASIDE-SPARROW

(subspecies of Seaside Sparrow)

DATE	
LOCATION	
REMARKS	

FOX SPARROW

Passerella iliaca

DATE	
LOCATION	
REMARKS	

SONG SPARROW *Melospiza melodia*	DATE
	LOCATION
	REMARKS

LINCOLN'S SPARROW *Melospiza lincolnii*	DATE
	LOCATION
	REMARKS

SWAMP SPARROW *Melospiza georgiana*	DATE
	LOCATION
	REMARKS

WHITE-THROATED SPARROW *Zonotrichia albicollis*	DATE
	LOCATION
	REMARKS

GOLDEN-CROWNED SPARROW *Zonotrichia atricapilla*	DATE
	LOCATION
	REMARKS

SPARROWS, JUNCOS

WHITE-CROWNED SPARROW
Zonotrichia leucophrys

DATE
LOCATION
REMARKS

HARRIS' SPARROW
Zonotrichia querula

DATE
LOCATION
REMARKS

DARK-EYED JUNCO "SLATE-COLORED"
Junco hyemalis

DATE
LOCATION
REMARKS

"OREGON" JUNCO
(subspecies of Dark-eyed Junco)

DATE
LOCATION
REMARKS

"WHITE-WINGED" JUNCO
(subspecies of Dark-eyed Junco)

DATE
LOCATION
REMARKS

"GRAY-HEADED" JUNCO *(subspecies of Dark-eyed Junco)*	DATE
	LOCATION
	REMARKS

YELLOW-EYED JUNCO *Junco phaeonotus*	DATE
	LOCATION
	REMARKS

McCOWN'S LONGSPUR *Calcarius mccownii*	DATE
	LOCATION
	REMARKS

LAPLAND LONGSPUR *Calcarius lapponicus*	DATE
	LOCATION
	REMARKS

SMITH'S LONGSPUR *Calcarius pictus*	DATE
	LOCATION
	REMARKS

152

LONGSPUR, BUNTINGS

CHESTNUT-COLLARED LONGSPUR *Calcarius ornatus*	DATE
	LOCATION
	REMARKS

SNOW BUNTING *Plectrophenax nivalis*	DATE
	LOCATION
	REMARKS

McKAY'S BUNTING *Plectrophenax hyperboreus*	DATE
	LOCATION
	REMARKS

	DATE
	LOCATION
	REMARKS

	DATE
	LOCATION
	REMARKS

BOBOLINK

Dolichonyx oryzivorus

DATE

LOCATION

REMARKS

RED-WINGED BLACKBIRD

Agelaius phoeniceus

DATE

LOCATION

REMARKS

TRICOLORED BLACKBIRD

Agelaius tricolor

DATE

LOCATION

REMARKS

EASTERN MEADOWLARK

Sturnella magna

DATE

LOCATION

REMARKS

WESTERN MEADOWLARK

Sturnella neglecta

DATE

LOCATION

REMARKS

BLACKBIRDS, GRACKLES

YELLOW-HEADED BLACKBIRD

Xanthocephalus xanthocephalus

DATE

LOCATION

REMARKS

RUSTY BLACKBIRD

Euphagus carolinus

DATE

LOCATION

REMARKS

BREWER'S BLACKBIRD

Euphagus cyanocephalus

DATE

LOCATION

REMARKS

GREAT-TAILED GRACKLE

Quiscalus mexicanus

DATE

LOCATION

REMARKS

BOAT-TAILED GRACKLE

Quiscalus major

DATE

LOCATION

REMARKS

COMMON GRACKLE

Quiscalus quiscula

DATE	
LOCATION	
REMARKS	

SHINY COWBIRD

Molothrus bonariensis

DATE	
LOCATION	
REMARKS	

BRONZED COWBIRD

Molothrus aeneus

DATE	
LOCATION	
REMARKS	

BROWN-HEADED COWBIRD

Molothrus ater

DATE	
LOCATION	
REMARKS	

ORCHARD ORIOLE

Icterus spurius

DATE	
LOCATION	
REMARKS	

ORIOLES

HOODED ORIOLE

Icterus cucullatus

DATE	
LOCATION	
REMARKS	

STREAK-BACKED ORIOLE

Icterus pustulatus

DATE	
LOCATION	
REMARKS	

SPOT-BREASTED ORIOLE

Icterus pectoralis

DATE	
LOCATION	
REMARKS	

ALTAMIRA ORIOLE

Icterus gularis

DATE	
LOCATION	
REMARKS	

AUDUBON'S ORIOLE

Icterus graduacauda

DATE	
LOCATION	
REMARKS	

NORTHERN ORIOLE "BALTIMORE" *Icterus galbula*	DATE
	LOCATION
	REMARKS

"BULLOCK'S" ORIOLE *(subspecies of Northern Oriole)*	DATE
	LOCATION
	REMARKS

SCOTT'S ORIOLE *Icterus parisorum*	DATE
	LOCATION
	REMARKS

	DATE
	LOCATION
	REMARKS

	DATE
	LOCATION
	REMARKS

BRAMBLING, FINCHES

BRAMBLING *Fringilla* *montifringilla*	DATE
	LOCATION
	REMARKS

ROSY FINCH *Leucosticte arctoa*	DATE
	LOCATION
	REMARKS

"GRAY- **CROWNED"** **ROSY-FINCH** *(subspecies of* *Rosy Finch)*	DATE
	LOCATION
	REMARKS

"BLACK" ROSY- **FINCH** *(subspecies of* *Rosy Finch)*	DATE
	LOCATION
	REMARKS

"BROWN- **CAPPED"** **ROSY-FINCH** *(subspecies of* *Rosy Finch)*	DATE
	LOCATION
	REMARKS

PINE GROSBEAK *Pinicola enucleator*	DATE
	LOCATION
	REMARKS

PURPLE FINCH *Carpodacus purpureus*	DATE
	LOCATION
	REMARKS

CASSIN'S FINCH *Carpodacus cassinii*	DATE
	LOCATION
	REMARKS

HOUSE FINCH *Carpodacus mexicanus*	DATE
	LOCATION
	REMARKS

RED CROSSBILL *Loxia curvirostra*	DATE
	LOCATION
	REMARKS

CROSSBILL, FINCHES, GOLDFINCH

WHITE-WINGED CROSSBILL *Loxia leucoptera*	DATE
	LOCATION
	REMARKS

COMMON REDPOLL *Carduelis flammea*	DATE
	LOCATION
	REMARKS

HOARY REDPOLL *Carduelis hornemanni*	DATE
	LOCATION
	REMARKS

PINE SISKIN *Carduelis pinus*	DATE
	LOCATION
	REMARKS

LESSER GOLDFINCH *Carduelis psaltria*	DATE
	LOCATION
	REMARKS

LAWRENCE'S GOLDFINCH *Carduelis lawrencei*	DATE
	LOCATION
	REMARKS

AMERICAN GOLDFINCH *Carduelis tristis*	DATE
	LOCATION
	REMARKS

EVENING GROSBEAK *Coccothraustes vespertinus*	DATE
	LOCATION
	REMARKS

HOUSE SPARROW *Passer domesticus*	DATE
	LOCATION
	REMARKS

EURASIAN TREE SPARROW *Passer montanus*	DATE
	LOCATION
	REMARKS

162

WEAVER FINCH

JAVA SPARROW *Padda oryzivora*	DATE
	LOCATION
	REMARKS

	DATE
	LOCATION
	REMARKS

	DATE
	LOCATION
	REMARKS

	DATE
	LOCATION
	REMARKS

	DATE
	LOCATION
	REMARKS

APPENDIX A

HAWAIIAN SPECIES

DARK-RUMPED PETREL

Pterodroma phaeopygia

DATE

LOCATION

REMARKS

BONIN PETREL

Pterodroma hypoleuca

DATE

LOCATION

REMARKS

BULWER'S PETREL

Bulweria bulwerii

DATE

LOCATION

REMARKS

WEDGE-TAILED SHEARWATER

Puffinus pacificus

DATE

LOCATION

REMARKS

CHRISTMAS SHEARWATER

Puffinus nativitatis

DATE

LOCATION

REMARKS

HAWAIIAN SPECIES

TOWNSEND'S SHEARWATER *Puffinus auricularis*	DATE
	LOCATION
	REMARKS

TRISTRAM'S STORM-PETREL *Oceanodroma tristrami*	DATE
	LOCATION
	REMARKS

HAWAIIAN GOOSE *Nesochen sandvicensis*	DATE
	LOCATION
	REMARKS

HAWAIIAN DUCK *Anas wyvilliana*	DATE
	LOCATION
	REMARKS

LAYSAN DUCK *Anas laysanensis*	DATE
	LOCATION
	REMARKS

HAWAIIAN HAWK
Buteo solitarius

DATE	
LOCATION	
REMARKS	

GRAY FRANCOLIN
Francolinus pondicerianus

DATE	
LOCATION	
REMARKS	

ERCKEL'S FRANCOLIN
Francolinus erckelii

DATE	
LOCATION	
REMARKS	

JAPANESE QUAIL
Coturnix japonica

DATE	
LOCATION	
REMARKS	

KALIJ PHEASANT
Lophura leucomelana

DATE	
LOCATION	
REMARKS	

HAWAIIAN SPECIES

RED JUNGLEFOWL *Gallus gallus*	DATE
	LOCATION
	REMARKS

COMMON PEAFOWL *Pavo cristatus*	DATE
	LOCATION
	REMARKS

HELMETED GUINEAFOWL *Numida meleagris*	DATE
	LOCATION
	REMARKS

GRAY-BACKED TERN *Sterna lunata*	DATE
	LOCATION
	REMARKS

BLUE-GRAY NODDY *Procelsterna cerulea*	DATE
	LOCATION
	REMARKS

WHITE TERN

Gygis alba

DATE	
LOCATION	
REMARKS	

CHESTNUT-BELLIED SANDGROUSE

Pterocles exustus

DATE	
LOCATION	
REMARKS	

ZEBRA DOVE

Geopelia striata

DATE	
LOCATION	
REMARKS	

HAWAIIAN CROW

Corvus hawaiiensis

DATE	
LOCATION	
REMARKS	

RED-VENTED BULBUL

Pycnonotus cafer

DATE	
LOCATION	
REMARKS	

HAWAIIAN SPECIES

JAPANESE BUSH-WARBLER *Cettia diphone*	DATE
	LOCATION
	REMARKS

MILLERBIRD *Acrocephalus familiaris*	DATE
	LOCATION
	REMARKS

ELEPAIO *Chasiempis sandwichensis*	DATE
	LOCATION
	REMARKS

WHITE-RUMPED SHAMA *Copsychus malabaricus*	DATE
	LOCATION
	REMARKS

KAMAO *Myadestes myadestinus*	DATE
	LOCATION
	REMARKS

OLOMAO

Myadestes lanaiensis

DATE	
LOCATION	
REMARKS	

OMAO

Myadestes obscurus

DATE	
LOCATION	
REMARKS	

PUAIOHI

Myadestes palmeri

DATE	
LOCATION	
REMARKS	

GREATER NECKLACED LAUGHING-THRUSH

Garrulax pectoralis

DATE	
LOCATION	
REMARKS	

MELODIOUS LAUGHING-THRUSH

Garrulax canorus

DATE	
LOCATION	
REMARKS	

HAWAIIAN SPECIES

RED-BILLED LEIOTHRIX *Leiothrix lutea*	DATE
	LOCATION
	REMARKS

COMMON MYNA *Acridotheres tristis*	DATE
	LOCATION
	REMARKS

KAUAI OO *Moho braccatus*	DATE
	LOCATION
	REMARKS

BISHOP'S OO *Moho bishopi*	DATE
	LOCATION
	REMARKS

JAPANESE WHITE-EYE *Zosterops japonicus*	DATE
	LOCATION
	REMARKS

RED-CRESTED CARDINAL *Paroaria coronata*	DATE
	LOCATION
	REMARKS

YELLOW-BILLED CARDINAL *Paroaria capitata*	DATE
	LOCATION
	REMARKS

YELLOW-FACED GRASSQUIT *Tiaris olivacea*	DATE
	LOCATION
	REMARKS

SAFFRON FINCH *Sicalis flaveola*	DATE
	LOCATION
	REMARKS

YELLOW-FRONTED CANARY *Serinus mozambicus*	DATE
	LOCATION
	REMARKS

172

HAWAIIAN SPECIES

COMMON CANARY *Serinus canaria*	DATE
	LOCATION
	REMARKS

LAYSAN FINCH *Telespyza cantans*	DATE
	LOCATION
	REMARKS

NIHOA FINCH *Telespyza ultima*	DATE
	LOCATION
	REMARKS

OU *Psittirostra psittacea*	DATE
	LOCATION
	REMARKS

PALILA *Loxioides balleui*	DATE
	LOCATION
	REMARKS

MAUI PARROTBILL *Pseudonester xanthophrys*	DATE LOCATION REMARKS

COMMON AMAKIHI *Hemignathus virens*	DATE LOCATION REMARKS

ANIANIAU *Hemignathus parvus*	DATE LOCATION REMARKS

KAUAI AKIALOA *Hemignathus procerus*	DATE LOCATION REMARKS

NUKUPUU *Hemignathus lucidus*	DATE LOCATION REMARKS

174

HAWAIIAN SPECIES

AKIAPOLAAU
Hemignathus munroi

DATE	
LOCATION	
REMARKS	

KAUAI CREEPER
Oreomystis bairdi

DATE	
LOCATION	
REMARKS	

HAWAII CREEPER
Oreomystis mana

DATE	
LOCATION	
REMARKS	

MAUI CREEPER
Paroreomyza montana

DATE	
LOCATION	
REMARKS	

MOLOKAI CREEPER
Paroreomyza flammea

DATE	
LOCATION	
REMARKS	

175

HAWAIIAN SPECIES

OAHU CREEPER *Paroreomyza maculata*	DATE
	LOCATION
	REMARKS

AKEPA *Loxops coccineus*	DATE
	LOCATION
	REMARKS

IIWI *Vestiaria coccinea*	DATE
	LOCATION
	REMARKS

CRESTED HONEYCREEPER *Palmeria dolei*	DATE
	LOCATION
	REMARKS

APAPANE *Himatione sanguinea*	DATE
	LOCATION
	REMARKS

176

HAWAIIAN SPECIES

POO-ULI

Melamprosops phaeosoma

DATE	
LOCATION	
REMARKS	

RED-CHEEKED CORDONBLEU

Uraeginthus bengalus

DATE	
LOCATION	
REMARKS	

LAVENDER FIRE-FINCH

Estrilda caerulescens

DATE	
LOCATION	
REMARKS	

ORANGE-CHEEKED WAXBILL

Estrilda melpoda

DATE	
LOCATION	
REMARKS	

BLACK-RUMPED WAXBILL

Estrilda troglodytes

DATE	
LOCATION	
REMARKS	

RED AVADAVAT

*Amandava
amandava*

DATE

LOCATION

REMARKS

**WARBLING
SILVERBILL**

*Lonchura
malabarica*

DATE

LOCATION

REMARKS

**NUTMEG
MANNIKIN**

Lonchura punctulata

DATE

LOCATION

REMARKS

**CHESTNUT
MANNIKIN**

Lonchura malacca

DATE

LOCATION

REMARKS

DATE

LOCATION

REMARKS

ACCIDENTAL SPECIES

WANDERING ALBATROSS *Diomedea exulans*					
SHORT-TAILED ALBATROSS *Diomedea albatrus*					
LAYSAN ALBATROSS *Diomedea immutabilis*					
SHY ALBATROSS *Diomedea cauta*					
YELLOW-NOSED ALBATROSS *Diomedea chlororhynchos*					
MURPHY'S PETREL *Pterodroma ultima*					
HERALD PETREL *Pterodroma arminjoniana*					
COOK'S PETREL *Pterodroma cookii*					
STREAKED SHEARWATER *Calonectris leucomelas*					
LITTLE SHEARWATER *Puffinus assimilis*					
WHITE-FACED STORM-PETREL *Pelagodroma marina*					
BRITISH STORM-PETREL *Hydrobates pelagicus*					
BAND-RUMPED STORM-PETREL *Oceanodroma castro*					
WEDGE-RUMPED STORM-PETREL *Oceanodroma tethys*					
RED-TAILED TROPICBIRD *Phaethon rubricauda*					
RED-FOOTED BOOBY *Sula sula*					
GREAT FRIGATEBIRD *Fregata minor*					
LESSER FRIGATEBIRD *Fregata ariel*					
CHINESE EGRET *Egretta eulophotes*					
LITTLE EGRET *Egretta garzetta*					
WESTERN REEF-HERON *Egretta gularis*					
SCARLET IBIS *Eudocimus ruber*					
JABIRU *Jabiru mycteria*					
WHOOPER SWAN *Cygnus cygnus*					
BEAN GOOSE *Anser fabalis*					
PINK-FOOTED GOOSE *Anser brachyrhynchus*					
LESSER WHITE-FRONTED GOOSE *Anser erythropus*					
BARNACLE GOOSE *Branta leucopsis*					
BAIKAL TEAL *Anas formosa*					
FALCATED TEAL *Anas falcata*					
SPOT-BILLED DUCK *Anas poecilorhyncha*					
WHITE-CHEEKED PINTAIL *Anas bahamensis*					
GARGANEY *Anas querquedula*					
COMMON POCHARD *Aythya ferina*					
WHITE-TAILED EAGLE *Haliaeetus albicilla*					
STELLER'S SEA-EAGLE *Haliaeetus pelagicus*					
ROADSIDE HAWK *Buteo magnirostris*					
EURASIAN KESTREL *Falco tinnunculus*					
NORTHERN HOBBY *Falco subbuteo*					
CORN CRAKE *Crex crex*					
PAINT-BILLED CRAKE *Neocrex erythrops*					
SPOTTED RAIL *Pardirallus maculatus*					

ACCIDENTAL SPECIES

EURASIAN COOT *Fulica atra*					
COMMON CRANE *Grus grus*					
DOUBLE-STRIPED THICK-KNEE *Burhinus bistriatus*					
NORTHERN LAPWING *Vanellus vanellus*					
GREATER GOLDEN-PLOVER *Pluvialis apricaria*					
MONGOLIAN PLOVER *Charadrius mongolus*					
COMMON RINGED PLOVER *Charadrius hiaticula*					
LITTLE RINGED PLOVER *Charadrius dubius*					
EURASIAN DOTTEREL *Charadrius morinellus*					
BLACK-WINGED STILT *Himantopus himantopus*					
NORTHERN JACANA *Jacana spinosa*					
COMMON GREENSHANK *Tringa nebularia*					
MARSH SANDPIPER *Tringa stagnatilis*					
SPOTTED REDSHANK *Tringa erythropus*					
WOOD SANDPIPER *Tringa glareola*					
GREEN SANDPIPER *Tringa ochropus*					
GRAY-TAILED TATTLER *Heteroscelus brevipes*					
COMMON SANDPIPER *Actitis hypoleucos*					
TEREK SANDPIPER *Xenus cinereus*					
LITTLE CURLEW *Numenius minutus*					
SLENDER-BILLED CURLEW *Numenius tenuirostris*					
FAR EASTERN CURLEW *Numenius madagascariensis*					
EURASIAN CURLEW *Numenius arquata*					
GREAT KNOT *Calidris tenuirostris*					
LITTLE STINT *Calidris minuta*					
TEMMINCK'S STINT *Calidris temminckii*					
LONG-TOED STINT *Calidris subminuta*					
SPOONBILL SANDPIPER *Eurynorhynchus pygmeus*					
BROAD-BILLED SANDPIPER *Limicola falcinellus*					
JACK SNIPE *Lymnocryptes minimus*					
EURASIAN WOODCOCK *Scolopax rusticola*					
BAND-TAILED GULL *Larus belcheri*					
BLACK-TAILED GULL *Larus crassirostris*					
SLATY-BACKED GULL *Larus schistisagus*					
WHITE-WINGED TERN *Chlidonias leucopterus*					
BLACK NODDY *Anous minutus*					
SCALY-NAPED PIGEON *Columba squamosa*					
ZENAIDA DOVE *Zenaida aurita*					
RUDDY GROUND-DOVE *Columbina talpacoti*					
KEY WEST QUAIL-DOVE *Geotrygon chrysia*					
RUDDY QUAIL-DOVE *Geotrygon montana*					
THICK-BILLED PARROT *Rhynchopsitta pachyrhyncha*					
COMMON CUCKOO *Cuculus canorus*					
ORIENTAL CUCKOO *Cuculus saturatus*					
ORIENTAL SCOPS-OWL *Otus sunia*					
MOTTLED OWL *Ciccaba virgata*					

ACCIDENTAL SPECIES

JUNGLE NIGHTJAR *Caprimulgus indicus*				
WHITE-COLLARED SWIFT *Streptoprocne zonaris*				
WHITE-THROATED NEEDLETAIL *Hirundapus caudacutus*				
COMMON SWIFT *Apus apus*				
FORK-TAILED SWIFT *Apus pacificus*				
ANTILLEAN PALM SWIFT *Tachornis phoenicobia*				
GREEN VIOLET-EAR *Colibri thalassinus*				
RUFOUS-TAILED HUMMINGBIRD *Amazilia tzacatl*				
PLAIN-CAPPED STARTHROAT *Heliomaster constantii*				
BAHAMA WOODSTAR *Calliphlox evelynae*				
BUMBLEBEE HUMMINGBIRD *Atthis heloisa*				
EARED TROGON *Euptilotus neoxenus*				
HOOPOE *Upupa epops*				
EURASIAN WRYNECK *Jynx torquilla*				
IVORY-BILLED WOODPECKER *Campephilus principalis*				
GREENISH ELAENIA *Myiopagis viridicata*				
NUTTING'S FLYCATCHER *Myiarchus nuttingi*				
LA SAGRA'S FLYCATCHER *Myiarchus sagrae*				
VARIEGATED FLYCATCHER *Empidonomus varius*				
LOGGERHEAD KINGBIRD *Tyrannus caudifasciatus*				
CUBAN MARTIN *Progne cryptoleuca*				
GRAY-BREASTED MARTIN *Progne chalybea*				
SOUTHERN MARTIN *Progne elegans*				
COMMON HOUSE-MARTIN *Delichon urbica*				
MIDDENDORFF'S GRASSHOPPER-WARBLER *Locustella ochotensis*				
LANCEOLATED WARBLER *Locustella lanceolata*				
WOOD WARBLER *Phylloscopus sibilatrix*				
DUSKY WARBLER *Phylloscopus fuscatus*				
RED-BREASTED FLYCATCHER *Ficedula parva*				
SIBERIAN FLYCATCHER *Muscicapa sibirica*				
GRAY-SPOTTED FLYCATCHER *Muscicapa griseisticta*				
SIBERIAN RUBYTHROAT *Luscinia calliope*				
STONECHAT *Saxicola torquata*				
RED-FLANKED BLUETAIL *Tarsiger cyanurus*				
EURASIAN BLACKBIRD *Turdus merula*				
EYEBROWED THRUSH *Turdus obscurus*				
DUSKY THRUSH *Turdus naumanni*				
FIELDFARE *Turdus pilaris*				
REDWING *Turdus iliacus*				
AZTEC THRUSH *Ridgwayia pinicola*				
BAHAMA MOCKINGBIRD *Mimus qundlachii*				
SIBERIAN ACCENTOR *Prunella montanella*				
GRAY WAGTAIL *Motacilla cinerea*				

ACCIDENTAL SPECIES

BLACK-BACKED WAGTAIL *Motacilla lugens*					
BROWN TREE-PIPIT *Anthus trivialis*					
OLIVE TREE-PIPIT *Anthus hodgsoni*					
PECHORA PIPIT *Anthus gustavi*					
BROWN SHRIKE *Lanius cristatus*					
YUCATAN VIREO *Vireo magister*					
BACHMAN'S WARBLER *Vermivora bachmanii*					
CRESCENT-CHESTED WARBLER *Parula superciliosa*					
GRAY-CROWNED YELLOWTHROAT *Geothlypis poliocephala*					
SLATE-THROATED REDSTART *Myioborus miniatus*					
FAN-TAILED WARBLER *Euthlypis lachrymosa*					
GOLDEN-CROWNED WARBLER *Basileuterus culicivorus*					
FLAME-COLORED TANAGER *Piranga bidentata*					
CRIMSON-COLLARED GROSBEAK *Rhodothraupis celaeno*					
YELLOW GROSBEAK *Pheucticus chrysopeplus*					
BLUE BUNTING *Cyanocompsa parellina*					
BLACK-FACED GRASSQUIT *Tiaris bicolor*					
WORTHEN'S SPARROW *Spizella wortheni*					
LITTLE BUNTING *Emberiza pusilla*					
RUSTIC BUNTING *Emberiza rustica*					
YELLOW-BREASTED BUNTING *Emberiza aureola*					
GRAY BUNTING *Emberiza variabilis*					
PALLAS' REED-BUNTING *Emberiza pallasi*					
COMMON REED-BUNTING *Emberiza schoeniclus*					
TAWNY-SHOULDERED BLACKBIRD *Agelaius humeralis*					
BLACK-VENTED ORIOLE *Icterus wagleri*					
COMMON CHAFFINCH *Fringilla coelebs*					
COMMON ROSEFINCH *Carpodacus erythrinus*					
EUROPEAN GOLDFINCH *Carduelis carduelis*					
ORIENTAL GREENFINCH *Carduelis sinica*					
EURASIAN BULLFINCH *Pyrrhula pyrrhula*					
HAWFINCH *Coccothraustes coccothraustes*					

APPENDIX C

LIFE LIST

1		47	
2		48	
3		49	
4		50	
5		51	
6		52	
7		53	
8		54	
9		55	
10		56	
11		57	
12		58	
13		59	
14		60	
15		61	
16		62	
17		63	
18		64	
19		65	
20		66	
21		67	
22		68	
23		69	
24		70	
25		71	
26		72	
27		73	
28		74	
29		75	
30		76	
31		77	
32		78	
33		79	
34		80	
35		81	
36		82	
37		83	
38		84	
39		85	
40		86	
41		87	
42		88	
43		89	
44		90	
45		91	
46		92	

LIFE LIST

93		139	
94		140	
95		141	
96		142	
97		143	
98		144	
99		145	
100		146	
101		147	
102		148	
103		149	
104		150	
105		151	
106		152	
107		153	
108		154	
109		155	
110		156	
111		157	
112		158	
113		159	
114		160	
115		161	
116		162	
117		163	
118		164	
119		165	
120		166	
121		167	
122		168	
123		169	
124		170	
125		171	
126		172	
127		173	
128		174	
129		175	
130		176	
131		177	
132		178	
133		179	
134		180	
135		181	
136		182	
137		183	
138		184	

LIFE LIST

#		#	
185		231	
186		232	
187		233	
188		234	
189		235	
190		236	
191		237	
192		238	
193		239	
194		240	
195		241	
196		242	
197		243	
198		244	
199		245	
200		246	
201		247	
202		248	
203		249	
204		250	
205		251	
206		252	
207		253	
208		254	
209		255	
210		256	
211		257	
212		258	
213		259	
214		260	
215		261	
216		262	
217		263	
218		264	
219		265	
220		266	
221		267	
222		268	
223		269	
224		270	
225		271	
226		272	
227		273	
228		274	
229		275	
230		276	

277		323	
278		324	
279		325	
280		326	
281		327	
282		328	
283		329	
284		330	
285		331	
286		332	
287		333	
288		334	
289		335	
290		336	
291		337	
292		338	
293		339	
294		340	
295		341	
296		342	
297		343	
298		344	
299		345	
300		346	
301		347	
302		348	
303		349	
304		350	
305		351	
306		352	
307		353	
308		354	
309		355	
310		356	
311		357	
312		358	
313		359	
314		360	
315		361	
316		362	
317		363	
318		364	
319		365	
320		366	
321		367	
322		368	

LIFE LIST

369		415	
370		416	
371		417	
372		418	
373		419	
374		420	
375		421	
376		422	
377		423	
378		424	
379		425	
380		426	
381		427	
382		428	
383		429	
384		430	
385		431	
386		432	
387		433	
388		434	
389		435	
390		436	
391		437	
392		438	
393		439	
394		440	
395		441	
396		442	
397		443	
398		444	
399		445	
400		446	
401		447	
402		448	
403		449	
404		450	
405		451	
406		452	
407		453	
408		454	
409		455	
410		456	
411		457	
412		458	
413		459	
414		460	

461		507	
462		508	
463		509	
464		510	
465		511	
466		512	
467		513	
468		514	
469		515	
470		516	
471		517	
472		518	
473		519	
474		520	
475		521	
476		522	
477		523	
478		524	
479		525	
480		526	
481		527	
482		528	
483		529	
484		530	
485		531	
486		532	
487		533	
488		534	
489		535	
490		536	
491		537	
492		538	
493		539	
494		540	
495		541	
496		542	
497		543	
498		544	
499		545	
500		546	
501		547	
502		548	
503		549	
504		550	
505		551	
506		552	

LIFE LIST

553		599	
554		600	
555		601	
556		602	
557		603	
558		604	
559		605	
560		606	
561		607	
562		608	
563		609	
564		610	
565		611	
566		612	
567		613	
568		614	
569		615	
570		616	
571		617	
572		618	
573		619	
574		620	
575		621	
576		622	
577		623	
578		624	
579		625	
580		626	
581		627	
582		628	
583		629	
584		630	
585		631	
586		632	
587		633	
588		634	
589		635	
590		636	
591		637	
592		638	
593		639	
594		640	
595		641	
596		642	
597		643	
598		644	

645		691	
646		692	
647		693	
648		694	
649		695	
650		696	
651		697	
652		698	
653		699	
654		700	
655		701	
656		702	
657		703	
658		704	
659		705	
660		706	
661		707	
662		708	
663		709	
664		710	
665		711	
666		712	
667		713	
668		714	
669		715	
670		716	
671		717	
672		718	
673		719	
674		720	
675		721	
676		722	
677		723	
678		724	
679		725	
680		726	
681		727	
682		728	
683		729	
684		730	
685		731	
686		732	
687		733	
688		734	
689		735	
690		736	

190

LIFE LIST

737		783	
738		784	
739		785	
740		786	
741		787	
742		788	
743		789	
744		790	
745		791	
746		792	
747		793	
748		794	
749		795	
750		796	
751		797	
752		798	
753		799	
754		800	
755		801	
756		802	
757		803	
758		804	
759		805	
760		806	
761		807	
762		808	
763		809	
764		810	
765		811	
766		812	
767		813	
768		814	
769		815	
770		816	
771		817	
772		818	
773		819	
774		820	
775		821	
776		822	
777		823	
778		824	
779		825	
780		826	
781		827	
782		828	

	Page
ACCENTOR, *Siberian*	180
AKEPA	175
AKIALOA, *Kauai*	173
AKIAPOLAAU	174
ALBATROSS, *Black-footed*	8
Laysan	178
Short-tailed	178
Shy	178
Wandering	178
Yellow-nosed	178
AMAKIHI, *Common*	173
ANHINGA	14
ANI, *Groove-billed*	76
Smooth-billed	75
ANIANIAU	173
APAPANE	175
AUKLET, *Cassin's*	69
Crested	70
Least	69
Parakeet	69
Rhinoceros	70
Whiskered	69
AVADAVAT, *Red*	177
AVOCET, *American*	49
BANANAQUIT	138
BEARDLESS-TYRANNULET, *Northern*	94
BECARD, *Rose-throated*	101
BITTERN, *American*	16
Least	16
BLACK-HAWK, *Common*	34
BLACKBIRD, *Brewer's*	154
Eurasian	180
Red-winged	153
Rusty	154
Tawny-shouldered	181
Tricolored	153
Yellow-headed	154
BLUEBIRD, *Eastern*	116
Mountain	116
Western	116
BLUETAIL, *Red-flanked*	180
BLUETHROAT	115
BOBOLINK	153
BOBWHITE, *Northern*	42
BOOBY, *Blue-footed*	12

	Page
Brown	12
Masked	12
Red-footed	178
BRAMBLING	158
BRANT	22
"Black"	22
BUDGERIGAR	74
BUFFLEHEAD	29
BULBUL, *Red-vented*	167
Red-whiskered	111
BULLFINCH, *Eurasian*	181
BUNTING, Blue	181
Gray	181
Indigo	141
Lark	146
Lazuli	141
Little	181
McKay's	152
Painted	141
Rustic	181
Snow	152
Varied	141
Yellow-breasted	181
BUSH-WARBLER, *Japanese*	168
BUSHTIT	110
"Black-eared"	110
CANARY, *Common*	172
Yellow-fronted	171
CANVASBACK	26
CARACARA, *Crested*	37
CARDINAL, *Northern*	140
Red-crested	171
Yellow-billed	171
CATBIRD, *Gray*	119
CHACHALACA, *Plain*	39
CHAFFINCH, *Common*	181
CHAT, *Yellow-breasted*	137
CHICKADEE, *Black-capped*	108
Boreal	109
Carolina	108
Chestnut-backed	109
Mexican	108
Mountain	108
CHUCK-WILL'S-WIDOW	82
CHUKAR	39

	Page											
COLLARED-DOVE, Eurasian	71											
CONDOR, California	31											
COOT, American	45											
Caribbean	45											
Eurasian	179											
CORDONBLEU, Red-cheeked	176											
CORMORANT, Brandt's	14											
Double-crested	13											
Great	13											
Olivaceous	14											
Pelagic	14											
Red-faced	14											
COWBIRD, Bronzed	155											
Brown-headed	155											
Shiny	155											
CRAKE, Corn	178											
Paint-billed	178											
CRANE, Common	179											
Sandhill	46											
Whooping	46											
CREEPER, Brown	111											
Hawaii	174											
Kauai	174											
Maui	174											
Molokai	174											
Oahu	175											
CROSSBILL, Red	159											
White-winged	160											
CROW, American	106											
Fish	107											
Hawaiian	167											
Mexican	106											
Northwestern	106											
CUCKOO, Black-billed	75											
Common	179											
Mangrove	75											
Oriental	179											
Yellow-billed	75											
CURLEW, Bristle-thighed	51											
Eskimo	50											
Eurasian	179											
Far Eastern	179											
Little	179											
Long-billed	51											
Slender-billed	179											

INDEX

	Page
DICKCISSEL	141
DIPPER, *American*	114
DOTTEREL, *Eurasian*	179
DOVE, *Inca*	72
Mourning	72
Rock	71
Spotted	72
White-tipped	73
White-winged	72
Zebra	167
Zenaida	179
DOVEKIE	67
DOWITCHER, *Long-billed*	56
Short-billed	56
DUCK, *American Black*	23
Harlequin	28
Hawaiian	164
Laysan	164
Masked	30
"Mexican"	24
Mottled	23
Ring-necked	26
Ruddy	30
Spot-billed	178
Tufted	26
Wood	23
DUNLIN	55
EAGLE, *Bald*	32
Golden	36
White-tailed	178
EGRET, *Cattle*	17
Chinese	178
Great	16
Little	178
Reddish	17
Snowy	17
EIDER, *Common*	27
King	27
Spectacled	27
Steller's	27
ELAENIA, *Greenish*	180
ELEPAIO	168
FALCON, *Aplomado*	37
Peregrine	37

	Page
Prairie	38
FIELDFARE	180
FINCH, Cassin's	159
House	159
Laysan	172
Nihoa	172
Purple	159
Rosy	158
Saffron	171
FIRE-FINCH, Lavender	176
FLAMINGO, Greater	19
FLICKER, "Gilded"	93
Northern	92
"Red-shafted"	93
"Yellow-shafted"	92
FLYCATCHER, Acadian	95
Alder	95
Ash-throated	98
Brown-crested	98
Buff-breasted	97
Cordilleran	96
Dusky	96
Dusky-capped	98
Fork-tailed	100
Gray	96
Gray-spotted	180
Great Crested	98
Hammond's	96
LaSagra's	180
Least	95
Nutting's	180
Olive-sided	94
Pacific-slope	96
Red-breasted	180
Scissor-tailed	100
Siberian	180
Sulphur-bellied	99
Variegated	180
Vermilion	97
Willow	95
Yellow-bellied	95
FRANCOLIN, Black	39
Erckel's	165
Gray	165
FRIGATEBIRD, Great	178
Lesser	178

INDEX

	Page											
Magnificent	15											
FULMAR, *Northern*	8											
GADWALL	25											
GALLINULE, *Purple*	45											
GANNET, *Northern*	13											
GARGANEY	178											
GNATCATCHER, *Black-capped*	115											
Black-tailed	115											
Blue-gray	115											
California	115											
GODWIT, *Bar-tailed*	52											
Black-tailed	51											
Hudsonian	51											
Marbled	52											
GOLDEN-PLOVER, *Greater*	179											
Lesser	47											
GOLDENEYE, *Barrow's*	29											
Common	29											
GOLDFINCH, *American*	161											
European	181											
Lawrence's	161											
Lesser	160											
GOOSE, *Barnacle*	178											
Bean	178											
"Blue"	21											
Canada	22											
Emperor	21											
Greater White-fronted	21											
Hawaiian	164											
Lesser White-fronted	178											
Pink-footed	178											
Ross'	21											
Snow	21											
GOSHAWK, *Northern*	33											
GRACKLE, *Boat-tailed*	154											
Common	155											
Great-tailed	154											
GRASSHOPPER-WARBLER, *Middendorf's*	180											
GRASSQUIT, *Black-faced*	181											
Yellow-faced	171											
GREBE, *Clark's*	7											
Eared	6											
Horned	6											
Least	6											
Pied-billed	6											

	Page
Red-necked	6
Western	7
GREENFINCH, *Oriental*	181
GREENSHANK, *Common*	179
GROSBEAK, *Black-headed*	140
Blue	140
Crimson-collared	181
Evening	161
Pine	159
Rose-breasted	140
Yellow	181
GROUND-DOVE, *Common*	73
Ruddy	179
GROUSE, *Blue*	40
Ruffed	41
Sage	41
Sharp-tailed	41
Spruce	40
GUILLEMOT, *Black*	67
Pigeon	68
GUINEAFOWL, *Helmeted*	166
GULL, *Band-tailed*	179
Black-tailed	179
Bonaparte's	59
California	60
Common Black-headed	59
Franklin's	59
Glaucous	62
Glaucous-winged	62
Great Black-backed	62
Heermann's	60
Herring	60
Iceland	61
Ivory	63
Laughing	59
Lesser Black-backed	61
Little	59
Mew	60
Ring-billed	60
Ross'	63
Sabine's	63
Slaty-backed	179
Thayer's	61
Western	61
Yellow-footed	61
GYRFALCON	38

INDEX

	Page												
HARRIER, Northern	33												
HAWFINCH	181												
HAWK, Broad-winged	34												
Cooper's	33												
Ferruginous	36												
Gray	34												
"Harlan's"	36												
Harris'	34												
Hawaiian	165												
Red-shouldered	34												
Red-tailed	35												
Roadside	178												
Rough-legged	36												
Sharp-shinned	33												
Short-tailed	35												
Swainson's	35												
White-tailed	35												
Zone-tailed	35												
HERON, Great Blue	16												
"Great White"	16												
Green-backed	18												
Little Blue	17												
Tricolored	17												
HOBBY, Northern	178												
HONEYCREEPER, Crested	175												
HOOPOE	180												
HOUSE-MARTIN, Common	180												
HUMMINGBIRD, Allen's	86												
Anna's	85												
Berylline	84												
Black-chinned	85												
Blue-throated	84												
Broad-billed	83												
Broad-tailed	86												
Buff-bellied	84												
Bumblebee	180												
Calliope	86												
Costa's	86												
Lucifer	85												
Magnificent	85												
Ruby-throated	85												
Rufous	86												
Rufous-tailed	180												
Violet-crowned	84												
White-eared	84												

	Page
IBIS, *Glossy*	18
Scarlet	178
White	18
White-faced	19
IIWI	175
JABIRU	178
JACANA, *Northern*	179
JACKDAW, *Eurasian*	106
JAEGER, *Long-tailed*	58
Parasitic	58
Pomarine	58
JAY, *Blue*	104
Brown	104
Gray	104
Gray-breasted	105
Green	104
Pinyon	105
Scrub	105
Steller's	104
JUNCO, *Dark-eyed*	150
"Gray-headed"	151
"Slate-colored"	150
"Oregon"	150
"White-winged"	150
Yellow-eyed	151
JUNGLEFOWL, *Red*	166
KAMAO	168
KESTREL, *American*	37
Eurasian	178
KILLDEER	48
KINGBIRD, *Cassin's*	99
Couch's	99
Eastern	100
Gray	100
Loggerhead	180
Thick-billed	99
Tropical	99
Western	100
KINGFISHER, *Belted*	88
Green	88
Ringed	88
KINGLET, *Golden-crowned*	114
Ruby-crowned	114

	Page
KISKADEE, *Great*	98
KITE, *American Swallow-tailed*	32
Black-shouldered	32
Hook-billed	31
Mississippi	32
Snail	32
KITTIWAKE, *Black-legged*	62
Red-legged	62
KNOT, *Great*	179
Red	53
LAPWING, *Northern*	179
LARK, *Horned*	101
LAUGHING-THRUSH, *Greater Necklaced*	169
Melodious	169
LEIOTHRIX, *Red-billed*	170
LIMPKIN	46
LONGSPUR, *Chestnut-collared*	152
Lapland	151
McCown's	151
Smith's	151
LOON, *Arctic*	5
Common	5
Pacific	5
Red-throated	5
Yellow-billed	5
MAGPIE, *Black-billed*	105
Yellow-billed	106
MALLARD	24
MANNIKIN, *Chestnut*	177
Nutmeg	177
MARTIN, *Cuban*	180
Gray-breasted	180
Purple	102
Southern	180
MEADOWLARK, *Eastern*	153
Western	153
MERGANSER, *Common*	30
Hooded	29
Red-breasted	30
MERLIN	37
MILLERBIRD	168
MOCKINGBIRD, *Bahama*	180
Northern	119
MOORHEN, *Common*	45

	Page													
MURRE, *Common*	67													
Thick-billed	67													
MURRELET, *Ancient*	69													
Craveri's	68													
Kittlitz's	68													
Marbled	68													
Xantus'	68													
MYNA, *Common*	170													
Crested	123													
NEEDLETAIL, *White-throated*	180													
NIGHT-HERON, *Black-crowned*	18													
Yellow-crowned	18													
NIGHTHAWK, *Antillean*	81													
Common	81													
Lesser	81													
NIGHTJAR, *Buff-collared*	82													
Jungle	180													
NODDY, *Black*	179													
Blue-gray	166													
Brown	66													
NUKUPUU	173													
NUTCRACKER, *Clark's*	105													
NUTHATCH, *Brown-headed*	111													
Pygmy	111													
Red-breasted	110													
White-breasted	111													
OLDSQUAW	28													
OLOMAO	169													
OMAO	169													
OO, *Bishop's*	170													
Kauai	170													
ORIOLE, *Altamira*	156													
Audubon's	156													
"Baltimore"	157													
Black-vented	181													
"Bullock's"	157													
Hooded	156													
Northern	157													
Orchard	155													
Scott's	157													
Spot-breasted	156													
Streak-backed	156													
OSPREY	31													
OU	172													

202

INDEX

	Page
OVENBIRD	134
OWL, *Barn*	77
Barred	79
Boreal	80
Burrowing	79
Elf	79
Flammulated	77
Great Gray	79
Great Horned	78
Long-eared	80
Mottled	179
Northern Hawk	78
Northern Saw-whet	80
Short-eared	80
Snowy	78
Spotted	79
OYSTERCATCHER, *American*	48
Black	48
PALILA	172
PARAKEET, *Canary-winged*	74
Monk	74
Rose-ringed	74
PARROT, *Red-crowned*	74
Thick-billed	179
PARROTBILL, *Maui*	173
PARTRIDGE, *Gray*	39
PARULA, *Northern*	129
Tropical	129
PAURAQUE	81
PEAFOWL, *Common*	166
PELICAN, *American White*	13
Brown	13
PETREL, *Black-capped*	8
Bonin	163
Bulwer's	163
Cook's	178
Dark-rumped	163
Herald	178
Mottled	8
Murphy's	178
PEWEE, *Greater*	94
PHAINOPEPLA	122
PHALAROPE, *Red*	57
Red-necked	57
Wilson's	57

INDEX

	Page
PHEASANT, *Kalij*	165
Ring-necked	39
PHOEBE, *Black*	97
Eastern	97
Say's	97
PIGEON, *Band-tailed*	71
Red-billed	71
Scaly-naped	179
White-crowned	71
PINTAIL, *Northern*	24
White-cheeked	178
PIPIT, *American*	121
Pechora	181
Red-throated	121
Sprague's	121
PLOVER, *Black-bellied*	47
Common Ringed	179
Little Ringed	179
Mongolian	179
Mountain	48
Piping	48
Semipalmated	47
Snowy	47
Wilson's	47
POCHARD, *Common*	178
POO-ULI	176
POORWILL, *Common*	81
PRAIRIE-CHICKEN, *Greater*	41
Lesser	41
PTARMIGAN, *Rock*	40
White-tailed	40
Willow	40
PUAIOHI	169
PUFFIN, *Atlantic*	70
Horned	70
Tufted	70
PYGMY-OWL, *Ferruginous*	78
Northern	78
PYRRHULOXIA	140
QUAIL, *California*	43
Gambel's	42
Japanese	165
Montezuma	42
Mountain	43
Scaled	42

	Page												
QUAIL-DOVE, *Key West*	179												
Ruddy	179												
RAIL, *Black*	44												
Clapper	44												
King	44												
Spotted	178												
Virginia	44												
Yellow	44												
RAVEN, *Chihuahuan*	107												
Common	107												
RAZORBILL	67												
REDHEAD	26												
REDPOLL, *Common*	160												
Hoary	160												
REDSHANK, *Spotted*	179												
REDSTART, *American*	134												
Painted	137												
Slate-throated	181												
REDWING	180												
REED-BUNTING, *Common*	181												
Pallas'	181												
REEF-HERON, *Western*	178												
ROADRUNNER, *Greater*	75												
ROBIN, *American*	118												
Clay-colored	118												
Rufous-backed	118												
ROSEFINCH, *Common*	181												
ROSY-FINCH, "*Black*"	158												
"*Brown-capped*"	158												
"*Gray-crowned*"	158												
RUBYTHROAT, *Siberian*	180												
RUFF	56												
SANDERLING	53												
SANDGROUSE, *Chestnut-bellied*	167												
SANDPIPER, *Baird's*	54												
Broad-billed	179												
Buff-breasted	56												
Common	179												
Curlew	55												
Green	179												
Least	54												
Marsh	179												
Pectoral	54												
Purple	55												

	Page
Rock	55
Semipalmated	53
Sharp-tailed	54
Solitary	49
Spoonbill	179
Spotted	50
Stilt	55
Terek	179
Upland	50
Western	53
White-rumped	54
Wood	179
SAPSUCKER, Red-breasted	90
Red-naped	90
Williamson's	90
Yellow-bellied	90
SCAUP, Greater	26
Lesser	27
SCOPS-OWL, Oriental	179
SCOTER, Black	28
Surf	28
White-winged	28
SCREECH-OWL, Eastern	77
Western	77
Whiskered	77
SEA-EAGLE, Steller's	178
SEASIDE-SPARROW, "Cape Sable"	148
"Dusky"	148
SEEDEATER, White-collared	143
SHAMA, White-rumped	168
SHEARWATER, Audubon's	10
Black-vented	10
Buller's	9
Christmas	163
Cory's	8
Flesh-footed	9
Greater	9
Little	178
Manx	10
Pink-footed	9
Short-tailed	10
Sooty	9
Streaked	178
Townsend's	164
Wedge-tailed	163
SHOVELER, Northern	25

INDEX

	Page
SHRIKE, *Brown*	181
Loggerhead	123
Northern	123
SILVERBILL, *Warbling*	177
SISKIN, *Pine*	160
SKIMMER, *Black*	66
SKUA, *Great*	58
South Polar	58
SKYLARK, *Eurasian*	101
SMEW	29
SNIPE, *Common*	56
Jack	179
SOLITAIRE, *Townsend's*	116
SORA	45
SPARROW, *American Tree*	144
Bachman's	143
Baird's	147
Black-chinned	145
Black-throated	146
Botteri's	143
Brewer's	145
Cassin's	143
Chipping	144
Clay-colored	144
Eurasian Tree	161
Field	145
Five-striped	146
Fox	148
Golden-crowned	149
Grasshopper	147
Harris'	150
Henslow's	147
House	161
"Ipswich"	147
Java	162
Lark	145
Le Conte's	147
Lincoln's	149
Olive	142
Rufous-crowned	144
Rufous-winged	144
Sage	146
Savannah	146
Seaside	148
Sharp-tailed	148
Song	149

	Page									
Swamp	149									
Vesper	145									
White-crowned	150									
White-throated	149									
Worthen's	181									
SPOONBILL, *Roseate*	19									
STARLING, *European*	123									
STARTHROAT, *Plain-capped*	180									
STILT, *Black-necked*	49									
Black-winged	179									
STINT, *Little*	179									
Long-toed	179									
Rufous-necked	53									
Temminck's	179									
STONECHAT	180									
STORK, *Wood*	19									
STORM-PETREL, *Ashy*	11									
Band-rumped	178									
Black	11									
British	178									
Fork-tailed	11									
Leach's	11									
Least	11									
Tristram's	164									
Wedge-rumped	178									
White-faced	178									
Wilson's	10									
SURFBIRD	52									
SWALLOW, *Bahama*	102									
Bank	103									
Barn	103									
Cave	103									
Cliff	103									
Northern Rough-winged	102									
Tree	102									
Violet-green	102									
SWAN, *Mute*	20									
Trumpeter	20									
Tundra	20									
Whooper	178									
SWIFT, *Antillean Palm*	180									
Black	83									
Chimney	83									
Common	180									
Fork-tailed	180									
Vaux's	83									

INDEX

	Page
White-collared	180
White-throated	83
TANAGER, Flame-colored	181
Hepatic	139
Scarlet	139
Stripe-headed	139
Summer	139
Western	139
TATTLER, Gray-tailed	179
Wandering	50
TEAL, Baikal	178
Blue-winged	24
Cinnamon	24
"Common"	23
Falcated	178
Green-winged	23
TERN, Aleutian	65
Arctic	65
Black	66
Bridled	65
Caspian	63
Common	64
Elegant	64
Forster's	65
Gray-backed	166
Gull-billed	63
Least	65
Roseate	64
Royal	64
Sandwich	64
Sooty	66
White	167
White-winged	179
THICK-KNEE, Double-striped	179
THRASHER, Bendire's	120
Brown	119
California	120
Crissal	120
Curve-billed	120
Le Conte's	120
Long-billed	119
Sage	119
THRUSH, Aztec	180
Dusky	180
Eyebrowed	180

	Page
Gray-cheeked	117
Hermit	117
Swainson's	117
Varied	118
Wood	117
TIT, Siberian	108
TITMOUSE, "Black-crested"	110
Bridled	109
Plain	109
Tufted	109
TOWHEE, Abert's	143
California	142
Canyon	142
Green-tailed	142
Rufous-sided	142
TREE-PIPIT, Brown	181
Olive	181
TROGON, Eared	180
Elegant	87
TROPICBIRD, Red-billed	12
Red-tailed	178
White-tailed	12
TURKEY, Wild	42
TURNSTONE, Black	52
Ruddy	52
TURTLE-DOVE, Ringed	72
VEERY	117
VERDIN	110
VIOLET-EAR, Green	180
VIREO, Bell's	124
Black-capped	124
Black-whiskered	126
Gray	124
Hutton's	125
Philadelphia	125
Red-eyed	125
Solitary	124
Warbling	125
White-eyed	124
Yellow-green	126
Yellow-throated	125
Yucatan	181
VULTURE, Black	31
Turkey	31

INDEX

	Page
WAGTAIL, Black-backed	181
Gray	180
White	121
Yellow	121
WARBLER, Arctic	114
"Audubon's"	130
Bachman's	181
Bay-breasted	133
Black-and-white	133
Black-throated Blue	130
Black-throated Gray	130
Black-throated Green	131
Blackburnian	131
Blackpoll	133
Blue-winged	127
"Brewster's"	127
Canada	136
Cape May	130
Cerulean	133
Chestnut-sided	129
Colima	128
Connecticut	135
Crescent-chested	181
Dusky	180
Fan-tailed	181
Golden-cheeked	131
Golden-crowned	181
Golden-winged	127
Grace's	132
Hermit	131
Hooded	136
Kentucky	135
Kirtland's	132
Lanceolated	180
"Lawrence's"	127
Lucy's	128
MacGillivray's	136
Magnolia	129
Mourning	135
"Myrtle"	130
Nashville	128
Olive	137
Orange-crowned	128
Palm	133
Pine	132
Prairie	132

	Page
Prothonotary	134
Red-faced	137
Rufous-capped	137
Swainson's	134
Tennessee	127
Townsend's	131
Virginia's	128
Wilson's	136
Wood	180
Worm-eating	134
Yellow	129
Yellow-rumped	130
Yellow-throated	132
WATERTHRUSH, Louisiana	135
Northern	135
WAXBILL, Black-rumped	176
Orange-cheeked	176
WAXWING, Bohemian	122
Cedar	122
WHEATEAR, Northern	116
WHIMBREL	51
WHIP-POOR-WILL	82
WHISTLING-DUCK, Black-bellied	20
Fulvous	20
WHITE-EYE, Japanese	170
WIGEON, American	25
Eurasian	25
WILLET	50
WOOD-PEWEE, Eastern	94
Western	94
WOODCOCK, American	57
Eurasian	179
WOODPECKER, Acorn	89
Black-backed	92
Downy	91
Gila	89
Golden-fronted	89
Hairy	91
Ivory-billed	180
Ladder-backed	91
Lewis'	89
Nuttall's	91
Pileated	93
Red-bellied	90
Red-cockaded	92
Red-headed	89

INDEX

	Page
Strickland's	91
Three-toed	92
White-headed	92
WOODSTAR, Bahama	180
WREN, Bewick's	112
"Brown-throated"	113
Cactus	112
Canyon	112
Carolina	112
House	113
Marsh	113
Rock	112
Sedge	113
Winter	113
WRENTIT	118
WRYNECK, Eurasian	180
YELLOWLEGS, Greater	49
Lesser	49
YELLOWTHROAT, Common	136
Gray-crowned	181

Join the Lab!

Our mission is to ensure that the next generation of birders enjoys the same diversity of bird species that we have today. We closely monitor bird populations, examine the causes of declining bird numbers, and promote the appreciation and conservation of birds. Your membership contribution will directly support vital research and conservation programs on behalf of birds. By working together, we can make a difference for future generations–of birds and birders alike.

Your benefits include:

Living Bird–our quarterly magazine loaded with information about all aspects of birdlife and illustrated with dozens of beautiful color photographs.

Birdscope, our newsletter, covers Lab activities, highlights study opportunities, and reports on our volunteer-based research programs.

*Many opportunities to participate in "Citizen Science" programs such as Project FeederWatch, Classroom FeederWatch, Birds in Forested Landscapes, and others.

*Discounts on our Home Study Course in Bird Biology and on any one of our field courses in birdsong recording, bird identification, and others.